The Ultimate Job Hunter's Guidebook

The Ultimate Job Hunter's Guidebook

THIRD EDITION

Susan D. Greene
Greene Marketing & Advertising

Melanie C. L. Martel
New Hampshire Technical Institute

Houghton Mifflin Company   Boston   New York

Executive Editor: George Hoffman
Associate Sponsoring Editor: Joanne Dauksewicz
Assistant Editor: Damaris R. Curran
Senior Project Editor: Fred Burns
Production/Design Coordinator: Jodi O'Rourke
Senior Manufacturing Coordinator: Sally Culler

Cover design: Harold Burch, Harold Burch Design, NYC

To the best of our knowledge, the information published in *The Ultimate Job Hunter's Guidebook* is correct and accurate at the time of publication. However, the text is intended only as a guide. Use your best judgment as related to your individual situation when applying the recommendations in this book.

Acknowledgments:
Permission to reprint the following materials is gratefully acknowledged:
Chapter 3: From Real Résumés & Cover Letters: Reprinted with permission.
Chapter 16: Figure, "Future Jobs Require More Education," from New Hampshire Job Notes: Reprinted with permission from *New Hampshire Job Notes*. Figure, "Crunch Time": Reprinted with permission from *New Hampshire Job Notes*.
Chapter 17: Excerpt from Ann Landers' column that appeared in *The Orlando Sentinel*, October 2, 1999, page E3: Permission to reprint granted by Ann Landers and Creators Syndicate. "The Victor" by C. W. Longenecker, as appeared in *The Orlando Sentinel*, September 26, 1998, page E3: "The Victor" by C. W. Longenecker.

Illustrations by Neverne Covington.

Printed in the U.S.A.

Library of Congress Catalog Card Number: 00-133813

ISBN: 0-618-05040-X

456789-DOC-04 03 02

CONTENTS

PREFACE   xiii

1 Planning Your Job Search   1

Job-Search Steps 2
1. **Conduct a Self-Assessment** 3
2. **Prepare Your Résumé** 3
3. **Target Potential Employers** 4
4. **Write Cover Letters** 4
5. **Obtain Letters of Recommendation** 5
6. **Fill Out Job Applications** 5
7. **Go to Interviews** 5
8. **Take Employment Tests** 5
9. **Organize and Survive the Job Hunt** 6
10. **Evaluate Job Offers** 6
11. **Get to Work** 6
12. **Plan Your Future** 6

2 Conducting a Self-Assessment   7

Know Yourself 8
Begin at the Beginning 8
Recognize Your Assets 10
Take Action to Be Your Best 12
Evaluate Your Priorities 13

Choose the Right Job for You 14

Set Career Goals 16

Try Job-Shadowing 18

Volunteer! 19

Take a Career Test 20

Call in the Professionals 20

3 Preparing Your Résumé   21

How to Write a Résumé 22
  Style and Impact 24
  Basic Elements of a Résumé 25
  Language of Résumés 27
  Résumé Dos and Don'ts 28
  Action Verbs for Résumés 30
  Skills Identification 32

Types of Résumés 33
  The Chronological Résumé 33
  The Functional Résumé 33

What to Do About Gaps in Your Job History 52

Résumé Alternatives 53

Résumé Software 54

Make Your Résumé Computer Friendly 54
  Using Keywords 56
  Posting Your Résumé 57

4 Targeting Potential Employers   58

Generate Job Leads 59
  Networking Chart 60
  Keeping Track of Your Contacts 62

Turn Dead Ends into Live Contacts 63

Read the Classifieds 63
  Finding *All* the Job Ads 64

Making Contacts at Job Fairs 65

Research Companies 67

Conducting Informational Interviews 70

Should You Relocate for a Job? 73

Long-Distance Job Hunting 74

5   Have You Considered . . . ?   76

Federal Jobs   77
  Types of Federal Jobs   77
  Why Consider a Federal Job?   77
  Finding Federal Jobs   77
  Check Out Local Government Positions, Too   79
Working for a Nonprofit Organization   79
Working for a Small Company   81
Starting Your Own Business   82
Taking a Different Job Path   84
Further Education   85

6   Taking Your Job Hunt On-Line   87

Pounding the Virtual Pavement   88
  The New Medium for Job Seekers   88
  What Is the Internet?   88
  Using the Internet to Job Hunt   88
  It's Fast; It's Convenient   88
  Show Employers You Know Your Way Around the Internet   89
  Accessing the Internet   89
  Get Wired, Get Hired   89
  Searching the Internet   93
  The Right Site   93

7   Writing Cover Letters   95

Elements of the Cover Letter   96
The Write Stuff   97
  Try It!   100
Alternative Letter-Writing Strategies   100
Types of Cover Letters   101
Sample Letters   101

8   Obtaining Letters of Recommendation   109

References Available upon Request   110
   Who Can Give You a Letter of Recommendation?   110
   How Do You Get a Letter of Recommendation?   110
   What Should a Letter of Recommendation Say?   111
   How Many Recommendations Are Enough?   111
   When Should You Submit Your Letters of Recommendation?   111

9   Filling Out Job Applications   115

The Application Form   116
   Typical Application Questions   117
Sample Employment Application   119

10   Interviewing   121

Prepare for the Interview   122
   Types of Interviews   123
Create a Good First Impression   125
   Rules of Business Etiquette   126
   Dress to Impress   127
   Presenting Yourself on the Telephone   128
   The Telephone Interview   130
How to Handle Interview Stress   132
   Put Things into Perspective   132
   Sweaty Palms Are Not a Crime   133
   Hide Your Nervousness   134
Questions Asked in Job Interviews   135
   Questions an Interviewer Might Ask You   135
   Illegal Interview Questions   138
   Questions to Ask an Interviewer   138
You've Got Personality   139
   Personal Profile Keys   139
   Professional Profile Keys   140
   Achievement Profile Keys   140

Mind Your Body Language 142

After the Interview: Follow Up 143
  Career Search Organization Chart 146

Nontraditional Ways to Get an Interview 147

Reasons for Unsuccessful Interviews 148

Handling Rejection 150
  The Right Frame of Mind 150

Ask for What You Want 151
  A Final Note on Follow-up 152

11 Passing the Test   153

Employment Tests 154
  Drug Testing of Job Applicants 154
  Skills Tests 154
  Psychological Tests 155
  Physicals 157
  Probation Period 157

12 Backdoor Your Way into a Job   158

Taking an Indirect Approach to Job Hunting 159
  Multiple Jobs for Experience and Contacts 159
  Temping 160
  Freelancing 162
  Entry-Level Positions 162
  Internships 163
  Volunteer Work 164

13 Organizing and Surviving the Job Hunt   166

Take Care of Yourself 167
  1. Think of Job Hunting as Your Job 167
  2. Practice Time Management and Self-Discipline 167
  3. Set Goals 168
  4. Find Outlets for Stress 169

Job Hunter's Do List 170
Job Hunter's Time Planner 171
Troubleshooting for Job Hunters 172

14 Evaluating Job Offers 175

Choose the Best Job for You 176
Negotiate Your Salary 178
The End Is in Sight 180
The Acceptance Letter 180
The Rejection Letter 181

15 Getting to Work 184

Your First Few Weeks on the Job 185
Your First Year on the Job 185
Tips for Working with Your Manager 189
Managing Relationships on the Job 190
Finding a Mentor 192
How You Will Be Evaluated 192
The Importance of Staying Current 193
Alternative Work Arrangements 194
When to Move On 195

16 Planning Your Future 197

Trends in the Work Force 198
Top Careers for the Twenty-first Century 200
Fast-Growing Occupations 200
The Unsung Benefits of the Two-Year Degree 202
Job Security—A Thing of the Past? 203
Where Do Jobs Come From? 204
A Changing Work Force 205
The New Rules for Career Success 206

17 You Can Do It! 210

Success Stories 211
Advice from Those Who've Made It 222

INDEX 225

PREFACE

Job hunting. Just the thought of it gives most of us an uneasy feeling. Where do you look? Whom should you call? What if you can't find something in your field? Whether you're a recent graduate, an experienced professional, or someone returning after a leave of absence from the job market, simply getting started can be a tremendous hurdle.

This book is designed to help you move past that initial inertia and get your career on track. Written in conversational language, this third edition of *The Ultimate Job Hunter's Guidebook* takes you through the steps necessary to define your goals, create a winning résumé, write effective cover letters, generate job leads, and interview with confidence. This book is short on theory and philosophy but long on straightforward, easy-to-follow advice. Our practical tips are intended to help you excel in your immediate job hunt as well as your career over the long term.

Much of *The Ultimate Job Hunter's Guidebook*, Third Edition, is dedicated to the all-encompassing question of how to find potential employers. We review the typical methods as well as propose many nontraditional strategies. We even offer advice on ways to "luck into" the right job.

The Ultimate Job Hunter's Guidebook, Third Edition, also gives detailed instruction on how to take advantage of the new technologies revolutionizing today's job market. Discover the resources of the Internet, like databases that provide employers with instant access to your résumé, on-line classified ads from around the country, and company profiles that make employer research easy. Whenever possible, we give specific Web-site addresses at which you can find additional information or resources on a particular subject.

Finally, we offer numerous success stories of people who've made it. Their career sagas are inspirational, motivational, and, most importantly, educational. From their stories you'll learn that no matter how challenging your job hunt may seem at first, with a little hard work and creativity you have the potential to accomplish your goals.

For more information on any of the subjects covered in *The Ultimate Job Hunter's Guidebook*, Third Edition, and links to related web sites, please visit the companion web site for this text at http://college.hmco.com.

Susan D. Greene
Melanie C. L. Martel

A Note on Using This Book

Remember that the key to using this text, and the key to a successful job hunt for that matter, is to gather as much information as possible and then to make a plan of action using your own best judgment and the advice of those who know you and your field well. The icons in this text are designed to help you quickly focus on an important area.

INTERNET

The Internet icon means that here is a shortcut in your on-line research. The sites we've identified will bring you up-to-date, meaningful information as you work your way through the job-hunt process.

KEY POINT

The key icon should draw your attention to a major point in the text. Take a moment to evaluate and think critically about each of these important messages and what they mean to your particular job hunt.

DIVE IN

The diver icon is intended to spur you into action. If your tendency is to hesitate and mull over ideas too long without acting upon them, use this icon as a reminder to get busy. Try out one of the new ideas mentioned in the text, perhaps revising it slightly to make it appropriate to your own career field and geographic location.

EXERCISE

The exercise icon indicates that you will have an opportunity to practice and fine tune a particular skill. No one is a born job hunter; each person could benefit from honing his or her readiness and abilities at certain job-hunting crossroads.

Acknowledgments

The authors would like to thank the people who have reviewed this text and the previous editions for their many valuable comments.

Susan Borovsky
DeVry Institute of Technology

Nicol Burnett
Harding Business College

Elaine DePasquale
Robert Morris College

Wendy Edson
Hilbert College

Tedd Farrar
Virginia College

Robert Greenberg
University of Tennessee

Melody Hunt
Indiana Business College

Donna Jarrett
Bradford School

John McCarty
Mansfield Business College

Johanna McDowell
ITT Technical Institute

E. Kathleen Pollack
Bryant and Statton College

Rebecca Simoneaux
Blair Junior College

Teresa Quesenberry
Blue Mountain Community College

Dwight Wilson
Indiana Business College

We Want to Hear from You

Please keep the following questions in mind as you use this text during your job hunt. How is your job hunt progressing? Which ideas and suggestions in the third edition of *The Ultimate Job Hunter's Guidebook* have been most helpful? Which subjects would you have liked to learn more about? What was enlightening? Motivating? Mystifying? Write down your comments, suggestions, and job-hunting success stories and send them to us:

Houghton Mifflin Company
College Business Division
222 Berkeley Street
Boston, MA 02116

Send e-mail messages to:

college_bus@hmco.com

We'll gladly read your feedback and use it to make the next edition of *The Ultimate Job Hunter's Guidebook* even better.

Susan D. Greene
Melanie C. L. Martel

The Ultimate
Job Hunter's
Guidebook

CHAPTER 1

Planning Your
Job Search

Job-Search Steps

1	Conduct a Self-Assessment

2	Prepare Your Résumé

3	Target Potential Employers

4	Write Cover Letters

5	Obtain Letters of Recommendation

6	Fill Out Job Applications

7	Go to Interviews

8	Take Employment Tests

9	Organize and Survive the Job Hunt

10	Evaluate Job Offers

11	Get to Work

12	Plan Your Future

■ 1. Conduct a Self-Assessment (see page 7)

The first step in job hunting is finding out about yourself and your desires. Decide what you'd really like to do. What are your skills and capabilities? A little soul-searching at the start of your job hunt can pay big dividends. After you've learned about yourself, you'll be better able to determine what type of employment you're seeking.

Research different fields to find a career that matches your skills and your desires. Visit your local library and your local college's career planning and placement office, and job-shadow people whose careers are potential options for you. If you are still unsure, continue to expand your base of information. Work on your self-evaluation with a career counselor, if necessary. Then try to gather more information about the demands of different careers. Choose one or two careers to start your research, and take some pressure off yourself by remembering that very few people stay in the same career for life. The job you're seeking now is only the first step in a series of career moves.

Next, think about the geographic location where you'd like to live and work. Would you consider relocating? How far? The answers to these questions will determine the boundaries of your job search. Consider all the facets of your life that will hinge on the location of your job: housing, commuting, schooling for you and your family, and relationships that will change with distance. After you've looked at these and other pertinent factors, map out your target job-search area. Be prepared to rethink your career focus or target area if you consistently hit dead ends.

■ 2. Prepare Your Résumé (see page 21)

If you were building a home, you'd use the very best tools available to you so that the process would be easier and the outcome would be better. Similarly, when you build your career, it is important to use quality tools. Examine all the résumés you can find. Rely on your best judgment, but take into account the advice of those who work in your desired field. Make decisions about which format, paper, type styles, and wording you prefer. Write a few rough drafts and get feedback from trusted friends and professionals. A neat, well-written, and error-free résumé will not only give you confidence throughout your job search but also get you in the door and provide you with the opportunity to sell yourself at the job interview. You may find it beneficial to develop several versions of your résumé tailored to the various jobs you'd consider. Additionally, an Internet version might be necessary if you plan to post your résumé on-line.

■ 3. Target Potential Employers (see page 58)

Who employs people with your skills? Which companies are best, and which positions within them are likely to fit you best? There are many places where you can look for answers to these questions.

For written material, start at the library. Check out manufacturing and industrial directories. Find the appropriate professional journals and do a periodic search (a librarian can help you) to see what current newspapers and magazines have to say about a particular company or a general career field. College placement offices often have information on local companies. The local chamber of commerce or professional and business associations can also provide you with helpful literature. You might also glean valuable information from the classified ads and the Yellow Pages. Use the Internet to find want ads and to research companies. There are numerous web sites listed in this book, and some time spent "surfing" will give you an idea of the scope of information available.

However, your most valuable source of information is people. Be persistent and thorough. Let everyone you know help with your job search. Ask questions of friends, relatives, and coworkers. See what you can learn from members of your church, health club, social organizations, or professional groups. Person-to-person contact will provide you with current information and the "inside scoop" on certain companies or careers. Talking with people is a great way to begin establishing your network. It is also valuable preparation for the interview and an increasingly important skill in the work place. This is also the point at which you could begin informational interviewing to learn specifics from established professionals.

All your reading and networking should pay off with a long list of possible employers. Narrow this list to employers who meet the requirements you set in the first phases of your job search. Set aside organizations that are outside your geographical range or that do not employ people in the type of position you seek.

Now that you have a strong working list, do a bit more research by writing or calling potential employers to request any public relations information, sales literature, or annual reports they are willing to send you. Use these materials or your telephone skills to learn the name of the person who makes the hiring decisions at each work place. This is usually the person who would be your supervisor. When possible, avoid sending materials to the human resources office; its primary function is to screen out applicants!

■ 4. Write Cover Letters (see page 95)

You have all your tools—self-assessment, résumé, and research—and now you are ready to use them. Write a cover letter (also called a letter of application) to each employer and mail it with your résumé. Your cover letter gives you the chance to state which position you are applying for, to mention your strong points, and to ask for an interview. You'll probably need to develop several versions and review your drafts with others to double check your wording and format. Be sure to address the cover letter to a specific person whenever possible. Remember that the best person to send your cover letter to is the person who would be your supervisor, not the human resources department.

■ 5. Obtain Letters of Recommendation (see page 109)

Written references can be extremely valuable in convincing an employer to hire you. References serve as third-party endorsements testifying to the quality of your work and character. You can obtain letters of recommendation from previous employers, teachers, or anyone else whom you've known professionally. It is never too early to start soliciting letters of recommendation.

■ 6. Fill Out Job Applications (see page 115)

Some employers may want you to come in and fill out a company application form before considering you for a job. This small step is your first chance to show the employer the quality of your work. Brush up on the information these forms require so that you'll feel comfortable when the time comes for you to complete one.

■ 7. Go to Interviews (see page 121)

When you receive that important phone call telling you the date of your interview, begin practicing your interviewing techniques. Prepare a list of personal and professional references to bring with you. Research the company so you can answer the interviewer's questions intelligently. Find the company web site and gather any literature they publish. Also prepare your own list of questions about the company and the job.

Arrive for your interview on time and looking your best. Be ready to answer the interviewer's questions with poise and confidence. Watch your body language, voice, and mannerisms.

Consider each interview a learning experience and be prepared to evaluate yourself after each one. Whatever you do, remember that your work is not finished once the interview is over. Think of ways to improve your job-hunting skills, and follow up the interview with thank-you notes and phone calls to remind the employer that you're interested.

■ 8. Take Employment Tests (see page 153)

Because the costs of hiring and training new employees are so high, employers continually seek ways to weed out bad candidates. Some of the employment tests you may encounter are drug tests, aptitude tests, psychological tests, and medical exams. A prepared job applicant will anticipate this step.

◼ 9. Organize and Survive the Job Hunt (see page 166)

Realize that your job hunt will progress more smoothly if you are organized. Keep notes on the people you've contacted and the next steps in your job search. Make do-lists and charts to keep all important data in front of you. Keep all your papers together in a folder so that neither a special document nor an opportunity will be lost. Note the time-management and organizational habits of those you consider to be successful.

Take time to assess your progress and, if necessary, try some new job-hunting strategies. Be sure to take care of your physical and emotional well-being. Job hunting can be stressful, and in order to reach your goals you must learn to make your stress work for you.

◼ 10. Evaluate Job Offers (see page 175)

Your job hunt may be over, but you now face a decision that will have a huge impact on your life. Carefully weigh all your options to make the career choice that is best for you.

◼ 11. Get to Work (see page 184)

The first few months on the job are often fraught with challenges as you meet new people and begin to learn what your specific responsibilities will be. You may want to adjust your work habits in order to fit in at your work place. You will need to hone your skills, take in a tremendous amount of information, and learn about the corporate culture of your new work place.

◼ 12. Plan Your Future (see page 197)

The twenty-first century will see dramatic changes in the U.S. labor force and economy. Whereas your goal should be on developing a career that is interesting and meaningful to you, knowing some of the trends may help you to better plan your future. Continue to research job outlooks and how these projections will impact your career choice and educational plans.

CHAPTER 2

Conducting a
Self-Assessment

Know Yourself

■ Begin at the Beginning

Perhaps you have always known what career is right for you. Maybe you have been one of the few lucky people who have had insight into your strengths, interests, and values. If so, you have already completed the first step of the job-search process—knowing yourself.

A common experience for beginning job hunters, however, is confusion, nervousness, and a lack of direction. The pressure is intense. The task, as many view it, is to choose the perfect career that will provide satisfaction for a lifetime. No wonder that some job hunters launch prematurely into a field that is not a good choice and does not, as becomes clear later, suit the job hunter's interests or abilities. Others spend excessive amounts of time and sweat exploring in an unfocused and unproductive way.

If you begin the pursuit of your next career armed with the knowledge of your strengths, interests, and values, you will improve your motivation and your chances for success. You will also find it easier to set realistic, achievable goals. The exercise below enlists the help of others to help you clarify your self-knowledge. It answers the questions:

- How do others see me?

- What do they see as my strengths?

- How can I apply these strengths to a career?

EXERCISE

Valued Perspectives

Before your job search can truly begin, you must be able to identify your personality strengths and your skills.

Step 1

Interview five people who know you well and whose opinions you value. First, ask each person to list ten words to describe you. (Be sure not to let participants see anyone else's responses.)

	Name #1	Name #2	Name #3	Name #4	Name #5
1.					
2.					
3.					
4.					
5.					
6.					
7.					
8.					
9.					
10.					

Step 2

Next list the words that tend to be repeated or you feel are especially accurate:

Step 3

Add any words that you think describe you that are not included in the above lists:

Step 4

Rank all the adjectives listed above in order of importance:

1. _____   6. _____
2. _____   7. _____
3. _____   8. _____
4. _____   9. _____
5. _____   10. _____

Step 5

Examine the common themes and patterns of these responses. Usually, at the very least, those who know you well will indicate whether your talents lie in dealing with people, data, or ideas. What seem to be the most common strengths listed by those you surveyed?

Step 6

Brainstorm for connections: How do these strengths translate into job skills? Although answering this question is difficult, it is essential.

For example, if your friends and family have all noted your outgoing personality or unflappable disposition, you might be well-suited for a career that involves working with the public in a sales capacity or service industry. If they've noted you are detail oriented and logical, you might begin exploring a career in computer programming or technical support.

You may need the assistance of a professor, a business professional in one of the fields you are considering, or a career counselor, but be sure to carefully examine the links between your strengths and their work-place applications.

How do these personality traits translate into job skills?

Or, worded another way, list three to five job skills here:

1. _____
2. _____
3. _____
4. _____
5. _____

This exercise may be helpful to refer to when you are writing a job objective, preparing for an interview, or just feeling unsure of your strengths.

■ Recognize Your Assets

We all know some things about ourselves that we like and some things that we wish we could change. It's important to focus on your good qualities as you go through life, especially when under the stress of job hunting.

EXERCISE

Fill out the following questionnaire and refer to it when you need a boost before
EXERCISE an interview.

1. My best personality trait is _____ .

2. The course in which I did best in school was _____ .

3. I am good at _____ .

4. A skill I mastered quickly is _____ .

5. What I like best about working is _____ .

6. Good things my teachers or employers have said about me include _____
   _____ .

7. I often receive compliments on _____
   _____ .

8. I have a special talent for _____
   _____ .

9. One obstacle I've overcome is _____
   _____ .

10. I received an award or recognition for _____
    _____ .

11. My most valuable work skill is _____
    _____ .

12. People will enjoy working with me because _____
    _____ .

Reexamine your responses above. Below, write a brief, specific example of a circum-
stance that illustrates your responses to the questions you've answered above. Focus
specifically on numbers:

5. _____

7. _____

8. _____

9. _____

11. _____

■ Take Action to Be Your Best

KEY POINT

When you feel good about yourself, others can sense your self-confidence. Probably no other quality will make you more marketable as you search for a job. Now is a good time to make some positive moves toward improving how you look and feel, as well as how you perform in the work place.

EXERCISE

EXERCISE

Read down this list and check off the actions that you would like to take. Then write down a strategy for how you plan to make a change. Remember that the first step in making a positive change is recognizing a problem. The next step is creating a specific plan to remedy it. (You may need additional space to develop your plans.)

Take a look at these four examples for ideas:

6. Speak more clearly — Read the front page of the newspaper aloud into a tape recorder for fifteen minutes each day. Listen to the tape alone or enlist the help of a partner. Try to improve your diction, speed, and pronunciation.

12. Become more outgoing — Join a professional organization. Attend regular meetings and make a point of speaking with three individuals each time.

14. Computer skills — Set the goal of adding one small, measurable skill to your computer expertise each week. Learn to do spreadsheets or attempt a new word-processing program. Start where you feel comfortable and visit your college's learning center, community education division, or local adult-education class to get more help.

15. Writing ability — Keep a journal. Free write in it for at least twenty minutes each day. Later, choose a piece to revise and polish what you have written as a completed essay.

Personal Improvements   **Strategy**

1. Exercise more   _____

2. Lose weight   _____

3. Improve my posture   _____

4. Smile more   _____

5. Upgrade my wardrobe   _____

6. Speak more clearly

7. Clean up my language

8. Stop smoking

9. Become a better listener

10. Improve my manners

11. Pay more attention to personal hygiene

12. Become more outgoing

13. Other: _____

Professional Improvements

14. Computer skills

15. Writing ability

16. Public speaking

17. Technical skills

18. Other: _____

■ Evaluate Your Priorities

As you progress in your career, moving from your first job up the ladder of success, you may find that your priorities change. They may be influenced by such variables as your economic needs, your marital status, your career goals, your desire for personal time, and your family needs.

Take a moment to consider what your priorities are in life. For example, if you're seeking your first job, your goal may likely be to obtain a position that will give you good training and serve as a steppingstone to more advanced positions. If you have young children, you may prefer a job that does not require any overtime or weekend hours so you can spend more time with your family.

EXERCISE

Look over the following list of job and personal variables. In the left-hand column, number them in order of priority to you. Renumber them in the right-hand column based on the priorities you anticipate having five or ten years down the road.

Priorities Now	Job and Personal Variables	Priorities in 5 to 10 Years
_____	Salary	_____
_____	Family (children/spouse/parents)	_____
_____	Personal time	_____
_____	Job location	_____
_____	Work-related travel	_____
_____	Potential for advancement	_____
_____	Commuting time	_____
_____	Friendly coworkers/boss	_____
_____	Job responsibilities	_____
_____	Personal hobbies	_____
_____	Prestige	_____
_____	Benefits	_____
_____	Vacation time	_____
_____	Retirement plan	_____
_____	Security/stability	_____
_____	Personal growth/fulfillment	_____
_____	Exposure to new skills	_____

Choose the Right Job for You

As you embark on your job hunt, it's important for you to clarify your thoughts about the type of position you might like and the type of company for which you'd like to work. Once you've answered these questions, you'll be better prepared to market yourself and to find jobs that most appeal to you.

EXERCISE

EXERCISE Answer the following questions and refer back to this questionnaire when you're evaluating a particular position to see if it meets your desires.

1. I want to work for a company with
   - ❏ under ten employees.
   - ❏ under one hundred employees.
   - ❏ several hundred employees.
   - ❏ several thousand employees.

2. It's important for me to be in a position with potential for advancement.
   - ❏ True   ❏ False

3. I want a job that requires
   - ❏ a lot of creativity.
   - ❏ some creativity.
   - ❏ no creativity.

4. I want a position with
   - ❏ a lot of responsibility.
   - ❏ minimum responsibility.

5. I want a job with the following hours:
   - ❏ nine to five.
   - ❏ part time.
   - ❏ flexible scheduling.
   - ❏ potential for overtime.

6. I want to work for a company that
   - ❏ promotes from within.
   - ❏ brings in new people regularly.

7. In doing my job, I think I would like to
   - ❏ juggle a variety of responsibilities.
   - ❏ be responsible for one main function.

8. I would like a job that involves working with
   - ❏ people.
   - ❏ data.
   - ❏ products.

9. I would like to work for a
   - ❏ public company.
   - ❏ private company.

10. I want to work for a company that is
    - ❏ growing rapidly.
    - ❏ maintaining its status quo.

11. I want to work for a company located
    - ❏ within walking distance of my home.
    - ❏ no more than a half-hour drive away.
    - ❏ no more than an hour drive away.
    - ❏ I will relocate for a job.

12. I want a position with
    - ❏ a lot of structure.
    - ❏ minimum structure and an informal environment.

13. I like work that is
    - ❏ routine.
    - ❏ full of variety.

14. I enjoy working
    - ❏ in teams and groups.
    - ❏ by myself.

15. I enjoy working with
    - ❏ my hands.
    - ❏ my mind.
    - ❏ both my hands and my mind.

16. I enjoy working with
    - ❏ computers.
    - ❏ machines.
    - ❏ neither computers nor machines.

17. I want to work for a company that
    - ❏ allows employees to dress casually.
    - ❏ requires employees to dress up.

18. I want a job that has
    - ❏ no or low stress.
    - ❏ medium stress.
    - ❏ high stress.

19. I want a job that entails
- ❏ no travel.
- ❏ some travel.
- ❏ lots of travel.

20. I enjoy work that involves
- ❏ talking on the phone.
- ❏ face-to-face interaction.
- ❏ mostly written correspondence.
- ❏ minimal interaction with coworkers and customers.

21. I want a job that requires a
- ❏ high school degree or equivalent.
- ❏ college degree.
- ❏ graduate degree.

22. I want to work in an environment that
- ❏ does not allow smoking.
- ❏ permits smoking in specified areas.
- ❏ allows smoking without restriction.

23. To me, opportunities for training are
- ❏ very important.
- ❏ somewhat important.
- ❏ not important.

24. I want to spend most of my work day
- ❏ outdoors.
- ❏ indoors.

25. I want to work for a company that stresses employee training.
- ❏ True   ❏ False

26. I want a position that pays in the following range:
$ _____ to $ _____ .

27. Medical benefits are important to me.
- ❏ True   ❏ False

28. I want to work for a company that encourages further education and offers tuition reimbursement.
- ❏ True   ❏ False

29. I want a job title with
- ❏ a lot of prestige.
- ❏ some prestige.
- ❏ Prestige is not important to me.

30. When I picture myself at work, I envision myself doing _____ , in an environment that is _____ , with supervision that could be described as _____ , and with coworkers who _____ _____ .

Set Career Goals

KEY POINT   Developing a sense of direction for your career is important both before you begin your job search and after you've landed a position. By setting goals, you can work toward meeting specific objectives, measure your success, and achieve a feeling of self-satisfaction.

EXERCISE

Fill in the following blanks with your current goals, your goals for five years from now, and your goals for ten years from now.

1. Type of job desired:

   Current goal _____

   Five-year goal _____

   Ten-year goal _____

2. Responsibilities you wish to have in your job:

   Current goal _____

   Five-year goal _____

   Ten-year goal _____

3. Skills you wish to master:

   Current goal _____

   Five-year goal _____

   Ten-year goal _____

4. Salary desired:

   Current goal _____

   Five-year goal _____

   Ten-year goal _____

5. Other accomplishments that would help you measure your success:

   Current goal _____

   Five-year goal _____

   Ten-year goal _____

Trying to brainstorm your goals may make it apparent that you need more information to continue. This is a good sign. If necessary, begin researching a few occupations to establish their potential.

List your questions about one of your potential careers here:

1. _____

2. _____

Write the questions that you have been forming about other career paths here:

1. _____

2. _____

Try Job-Shadowing

Job-shadowing is an excellent way to investigate your career options. If you'd like to know more about a particular job, why not spend a day or two observing someone at work in your chosen field? A job-shadowing opportunity requires time and effort to set up, but it may be the best way to ascertain that your field of interest is truly suited to your skills, needs, and wants.

DIVE IN

First, find a contact person who works in your targeted career field. Locate someone who is willing to "show you the ropes" and let you follow him or her through an average day. Together, decide on a date when you can observe that person's daily work routine in person.

Make it clear to him or her that you don't plan to interfere in any way. Remain a silent, unobtrusive "shadow": listen and observe. This is not the time to ask for a job, although you may want to make note of contact names for the future.

If you are persistent and smart enough to set up a job-shadowing day or two, you'll find your efforts will be amply rewarded. The insight you'll gain by observing the work place and employee duties firsthand will give you a real taste of the field and a sense of whether it is right for you.

Finally, be sure to follow up your job-shadowing days with thank-you notes to all those who shared their time or expertise with you. Make lists of questions that you still need to research, reevaluate the pros and cons of the career if necessary, and also write down contact names that might be useful in the future. You

INTERNET

may also want to check out the *Occupational Outlook Handbook,* available at most libraries and on the Internet at www.bls.gov/ocohome.htm. It includes detailed profiles of hundreds of the most popular careers, based on interviews with people in those fields.

EXERCISE

EXERCISE

After you have tried job-shadowing for a day, write a brief summary of what you have learned. What were the job duties you observed? What about the job appealed to you most? What aspects of the job did you dislike? What surprised you the most about what you saw?

A career counselor can help you to focus your career goals. (© Kathy Sloane/Photo Researchers, Inc.)

Volunteer!

One of the best ways to get to know yourself while contributing to your community is by performing volunteer work. What volunteer work have you done? What have you learned from those experiences? If you haven't ever tried this particular method for self-discovery, now may be the time to start.

Human service agencies have a tremendous need for volunteers. Many different businesses and educational institutions would also gladly grant you exposure to the field in exchange for some of your time. People at these sites can also provide you with networking leads and references as you progress in your job search.

Take a Career Test

For some, taking the time to complete an aptitude test or an interest inventory at the start of a job search can be an eye-opening investment in the future. The most common tests are the Myers-Briggs, the Strong Interest Inventory, or a combination of the two. All of the exams ask you questions to gauge your likes, dislikes, and strengths. But remember, the tests are just another tool to help you do a self-assessment. They will enable you to narrow your choices by ruling out occupations that would be a wrong fit. They also point out career possibilities you might not have considered.

Many places offer these types of tests. In general, psychologists, outplacement centers, career coaches, universities, colleges, and even some high schools have them available.

Call in the Professionals

Career counselors and career coaches can be extremely helpful in helping you focus your career goals. These types of professionals can be found on most college campuses and in most cities. Consult your student handbook, your phone book, or an academic advisor. You can also find experienced career counselors through several Web sites. Most of these counselors provide their services via phone and e-mail. Just be sure you understand the fee structure before engaging their services.

INTERNET

Wall Street Journal (www.careersesj.com): Affiliated with Career Development Services, a nonprofit center in Rochester, N.Y., this site allows you to schedule a personal phone session with a career counselor.

The Five O'Clock Club (www.fiveoclockclub.com): This is a national career-counseling network that features a specialized approach to job searches. Fill out the profile questionnaire and you'll soon receive referrals for two career coaches who have an affinity for your special needs.

Career Counselors Consortium (www.careercc.org): This site features a directory of a group of New York–area career counselors. Issues they can deal with are: job searches, career choices, on-the-job difficulties, and skills assessments.

Career Experience (www.careerexperience.com): Send your questions to this group of counselors based in Canada and get an on-line answer usually within forty-eight hours. Services include résumé reviews, career assessments, and work-crisis responses.

CHAPTER 3

Preparing Your Résumé

How to Write a Résumé

How much time do you suppose the average employer spends looking at a résumé?

❏ fifteen minutes

❏ five minutes

❏ one minute

❏ thirty seconds

The correct answer is thirty seconds!

Remember, there is a lot of mystique and fear behind writing résumés. Once you know the basics, however, there is no reason you can't create a terrific résumé of your own.

Focus on the fact that your résumé is a tool to get you to the interview stage. It should present a concise, positive picture of your career goal, your education, and your experience.

EXERCISE

Check Your Résumé Savvy

True or False?

_____ **1.** It is never acceptable to use lime green résumé paper.

_____ **2.** One of the most effective ways to draw attention to a certain part of your résumé is to leave space around it.

_____ **3.** The most important thing an employer should remember after reading your résumé is your experience.

_____ **4.** The descriptions of skills listed in résumés must be written in complete sentences.

_____ **5.** If your health is excellent, you should mention that fact at the top of your résumé.

Multiple-Choice

1. Résumé software can
   a. create a generic looking résumé.
   b. be a good starting point when drafting a resume.
   c. be customized for different employers.
   d. do all of the above.

2. When the job experience section of a résumé is constructed to highlight the dates of the applicant's employment, that format is called
   a. a functional résumé.
   b. a chronological résumé.
   c. an abstract résumé.
   d. an electronic résumé.

3. An applicant's high school should be listed on the résumé if
   a. the applicant has not yet been accepted into a college or university.
   b. the applicant has graduated two to three years ago.
   c. the applicant has demonstrated some exceptional skill or talent during high school.
   d. all of the above conditions apply.

4. As a rule, the résumé of a person with less than five years full-time work experience should be
   a. one page long.
   b. two pages long.
   c. three pages long.
   d. written in paragraph form to expand upon the limited experience.

5. The average employer looks at a résumé for
   a. fifteen minutes.
   b. five minutes.
   c. one minute.
   d. thirty seconds.

The answers to these questions can be found on the following pages. The expanded explanations for the correct answers can be found throughout the chapter. Some responses may surprise you, but all should help you focus your reading on résumé preparation.

Answers to the Check Your Résumé Savvy Quiz

True or False

1. *False.* In certain liberal or highly creative fields, outrageous résumés are acceptable and may even be welcome! However, most traditional, conservative professions require a traditional résumé.

2. *True.* Sometimes less is more. Try not to overwhelm your reader with an overly "busy" résumé, full of too much bold print or crammed with too many different fonts and excessive graphics. Use a few different tools judiciously to carefully call your reader's attention to the key headings and the job titles or dates you wish to highlight.

3. *False.* The most important thing an employer needs to keep in mind after reading your résumé is your name. Without that recollection, all the other information is useless.

4. *False.* The résumé is designed to convey the most relevant information in the most condensed format possible. For this reason, it is important to use telegraphic phrases, starting with carefully chosen action verbs, to describe your skills.

5. *False.* Years ago listing one's health as "excellent" was an accepted résumé practice. These days, this phrase is unnecessary.

Multiple-Choice

1. The correct answer is *d.* Some novice job hunters become so enamored of new job-hunting technology that they forget that creating a résumé that is unique to your skills, education, and objectives still takes work.

2. The correct answer is *b,* chronological résumé. Be sure to examine many different résumé formats to decide if and how to highlight the dates of your employment experience.

3. The correct answer is *d.* As a rule, do not list your high school unless you are a recent graduate who has not yet matriculated into a degree program. If you had special work experience during high school or if you demonstrated leadership skills or athletic or academic talent, then you may want to include these facts on your résumé. Weigh the decision to list your high school skills against the fact that they may flag an employer to examine your youth or lack of experience.

4. The correct answer is *a.* A well-written one-page résumé is almost always the best choice for those with limited employment experience.

5. The correct answer is *d,* thirty seconds! This simple fact highlights how important the "details" of résumé preparation are. The lack of errors, the quality of the paper, and the neatness of the layout all take on unusual significance.

■ Style and Impact

Because an employer looks at your résumé so quickly, some of the smallest details take on major importance.

Paper. The feel of your résumé in the prospective employer's hand conveys one of the first messages about you. Flimsy, shiny, unsubstantial paper sends a negative message. For this reason, avoid onion skin or shiny photocopy paper. The paper you choose should be sturdy and professional. Choose quality paper that has some weight and is marked "letterhead" or "résumé stock."

The color of the paper also sends a message. In most cases, you will want your résumé to appear conservative and professional. White, off-white, beige, or light gray paper is fine. Some people choose to produce their résumés on light blue paper. Generally, the more conservative the business, the more conservative the color of the résumé. Hot pink might work well for a person applying for a position in advertising, but white would be better for someone applying for work in a bank. Again, unless you're trying to make a special point about your creativity, the paper should be a standard 8½″ × 11″. Finally, match your résumé paper to the cover-letter stock and envelopes to give a unified, consistent look.

Format. Because that first glance will be a quick one, you need to be sure that your most important points will stand out immediately.

How do you make a part of your résumé stand out while ensuring that the whole page is still easily readable? Think of the techniques that advertisers have used successfully for years:

- **White space.** Notice how the white space around a word catches your eye. Leave double or triple spacing above and below your name. Place headings in the center of a line. Put dates out in a margin. Readers are more apt to read a page with lots of white space than one crammed with text.

- **Capitalization.** Use it for headings or job titles.

- **Underlining or italics.** This is also a good way to make job titles stand out.

- **Bold print.** It can add a nice touch to your name.

- **Punctuation.** Stars and bullets sometimes help draw the eye to items in a list.

Whatever techniques you use to organize and highlight your résumé, be sure that your layout is neat, consistent, and appealing to the eye. Study as many different résumés as you can to see what appeals to you.

◾ Basic Elements of a Résumé

The parts of a résumé can be arranged to illustrate your best assets. The heading and job objective usually appear at the top of the page in that order. References usually appear at the bottom. If your education is more impressive than your experience, you might put it nearer the top of the page, and vice versa.

KEY POINT

Heading. This is one of the most important elements of your résumé. Include your name (which should stand out above all else), your address (both permanent and temporary), your e-mail address, and your phone number.

Objective. You might also call this "Job Objective" or "Career Objective." Write a one-sentence explanation of the type of position you are seeking. It usually appears beneath your name and address. Your objective should be as specific as possible and should not include your future career or educational plans. Note a specific job title, skills you'd like to use, and/or the location or size of the company for which you'd like to work. You can (and should) change your objective to fit the job you're applying for. If you cannot narrow down your objective, omit it.

Education. Include all the colleges you've attended, their names and addresses, and any degrees you have received. Give the dates you completed college or the date you expect to receive your degree. Under this heading, you should also be sure to list any certificates you've received and seminars or training programs you've completed. Some people also note special honors and awards, such as making the dean's list. If you've been accepted into a college, it is understood that you graduated high school, so there's no need to list it.

If you wish to stress portions of your education that are especially relevant or current, you might also include a subheading titled "Important Courses" or "Relevant Courses." Under this category, you list all classes you've taken that will be of special interest to the employer (computer classes are especially important). This section is useful if your education is more suitable to your objective than your work experience is.

Experience. This can also be called "Work Experience," "Employment Experience," or "Experience and Skills." Here you must give your previous employers, their cities and states, the dates you were employed, and the position you held with them. You may have to create your own job title if you didn't have an official one.

If your paid employment experience is limited, consider describing your volunteer work, internships, or practicums. List them just like your other work experience, but add the word *volunteer* or *intern* in parentheses.

Summary of skills. Some people include a brief paragraph outlining any special skills they have that might not be apparent in their job description. "Type 70 words per minute," "Thorough knowledge of Excel and MSWord," and "Fluent in French" are sample phrases that might appear in a summary of skills. Again, if your computer skills are extensive, this heading is a must. List it at the top of your résumé.

Activities and interests. You may choose to create a section on your résumé to demonstrate your interests outside of school or work. Some employers like to see an applicant who is well-rounded. However, be aware that some may view this information as frivolous or irrelevant. Be careful not to include any activity that may rule you out as a candidate.

References. For your résumé, it is sufficient to write "Available upon request" or "Furnished upon request." Be sure you can name three to five people who have observed your work habits and can speak about your character. Most people will not mind being a reference, but be sure you ask only those who will speak in the most glowing terms. Compile a list of their names, addresses, and phone numbers. You might also want to explain the nature of their relationship to you. Employers that request your list of references are definitely interested in you. (See more on letters of recommendation on page 109.)

■ Language of Résumés

The language used in résumés is unlike the language used in any other document. Your goal is to create a written summation of your skills, capabilities, and experience that is as brief as possible without omitting any of your strengths.

1. **Use action verbs.** Describe your duties with strong verbs—for example, *coordinated, delegated, trained,* or *supervised.*

2. **Do not use "I."** Each description of your responsibilities should begin with a verb.

3. **Use telegraphic phrases.** The "sentences" on your résumé should sound like the wording of a telegram. All unnecessary words should be left out. Words like *the, and,* and *so* can often be left out and the remaining fragment will still make sense. Notice the language in the sample résumés on pages 35–48. Each phrase starts with an action verb and ends with a period. For example, someone who has held a position as a customer service representative might write this:

Assisted customers with questions and complaints. Completed weekly reports. Provided material and assistance for production of monthly newsletters.

Remember that you can list your skills in the order of importance to your prospective employer, not necessarily in the order that you used these skills at your former work place.

What Not to Write on Your Résumé . . .

Here's a humorous collection of sentences that were found on real résumés. (They were submitted by various human resource departments.)

- I have lurnt Word Perfect 6.0 computor and spreasheet progroms.

- Received a plague for Salesperson of the Year.

- Failed bar exam with relatively high grades

- Marital status: single: Unmarried. Unengaged. Uninvolved. No commitments.

- Personal interests: donating blood. Fourteen gallons so far.

- Note: Please don't misconstrue my 14 jobs as "job-hopping." I have never quit a job.

- Marital status: often. Children: various.

- Finished eighth in my class of ten.

- References: none. I've left a path of destruction behind me.

4. **Use few abbreviations.** Abbreviating words may seem easy, but it's best to avoid this habit. Very few abbreviations are understandable to all readers, so use only the most common: "St.," "Rd.," and the letters of your degree, "A.S.," "B.S.," and so on. But, if you are applying for a new position in a field in which you previously worked, you may use some abbreviations that are common in that profession. When in doubt, write it out.

5. **Use numbers that favor you.** It is fine to write "Completed opening and closing procedures of cash drawer." It is even better to add "Handled $15,000 in daily cash receipts" or "Trained 10 other employees." Being specific will enhance your credibility.

■ Résumé Dos and Don'ts

Do

1. Use the best type of paper you can find. (Résumé, cover-letter, and envelope paper should match.)

2. Use strong action verbs to describe your skills. (See pp. 30–31 for a complete listing.)

3. List all of your accomplishments, including important courses, volunteer work, internships, relevant interests, and professional affiliations.

4. Arrange your résumé to show off your assets. Which heading should go first? Education? Experience?

5. Make it perfect. This is a cardinal rule of résumé writing.

6. Keep the résumé to one page, two if you've had extensive experience.

7. Use telegraphic phrases.

8. Proofread carefully. Ensure that your grammar and spelling are impeccable.

9. Consider having your résumé professionally typed and printed.

10. Experiment with several different formats and layouts. Are your skills best highlighted using the functional or chronological format? (See p. 33.)

Don't

1. Exceed one page unless you've had the experience to merit the additional pages. (Many employers only look at the first page anyway.)

2. Be wordy.

3. Use "I."

4. Use abbreviations, except for the most common ones.

5. Handwrite your résumé or cover letter.

Arrange your résumé to show off your assets. Experiment with several different formats and layouts to determine the best presentation. (© David Young-Wolff/PhotoEdit)

6. Use unusual paper, type, ink, or formats unless you're trying to make a special statement about your creativity.

7. Include any personal data such as height, weight, or marital status. If this information is pertinent to the duties of the job, the employer will request it later.

8. Include any information that could possibly be used to eliminate you as a candidate. Be especially careful to omit information about your religious or political affiliations.

9. Ruin a beautiful résumé by using a low-quality printer or reproducing it on a dirty copier. Take a moment to clean the copier glass to prevent blotches on your final copy.

10. Keep your résumé to yourself. Solicit opinions about your résumé from a variety of people you trust. Use their feedback to create a dazzling finished product.

■ Action Verbs for Résumés

Skim the list below to see whether any of these action verbs would be appropriate on your résumé. Remember that when describing your tasks in your current job, you should use verbs in the present tense. When describing previous positions, use verbs in the past tense.

Accelerated	Clarified	Decided	Experimented
Accomplished	Classified	Defined	Explained
Achieved	Coached	Delegated	Expressed
Acquired	Collected	Demonstrated	Extended
Acted as	Commanded	Designed	Extracted
Activated	Commended	Detected	Facilitated
Adapted	Communicated	Determined	Fashioned
Addressed	Compared	Developed	Filed
Administered	Compiled	Devised	Financed
Advanced	Completed	Diagnosed	Fixed
Advised	Composed	Directed	Focused
Allocated	Compressed	Discovered	Followed (up)
Analyzed	Computed	Dispensed	Forecasted
Answered	Conceived	Displayed	Formed
Applied	Conceptualized	Distributed	Formulated
Appointed	Condensed	Documented	Founded
Approved	Conducted	Drafted	Functioned
Arbitrated	Conferred	Earned	Gained
Arranged	Conserved	Edited	Gathered
Ascertained	Consigned	Eliminated	Generated
Assembled	Consolidated	Employed	Governed
Assigned	Constructed	Enacted	Guided
Assimilated	Consulted	Encouraged	Handled
Assisted	Contacted	Enforced	Headed
Assumed	Contracted	Engineered	Hired
Assured	Contributed	Enhanced	Identified
Attained	Controlled	Enlisted	Illustrated
Attended	Converted	Ensured	Implemented
Augmented	Cooperated	Entered	Improved
Balanced	Coordinated	Equipped	Improvised
Bargained	Correlated	Established	Increased
Bought	Corroborated	Estimated	Influenced
Brought (about)	Counseled	Evaluated	Informed
Budgeted	Created	Examined	Initiated
Built	Culminated in	Exchanged	Innovated
Calculated	Cultivated	Executed	Inspected
Chaired	Cut	Expanded	Inspired
Charted	Dealt	Expedited	Installed

Instilled
Instituted
Instructed
Insured
Interacted
Interfaced
Interpreted
Interviewed
Introduced
Invented
Investigated
Judged
Justified
Kept
Launched
Lectured
Led
Lifted
Located
Logged
Lowered
Maintained
Managed
Marketed
Mastered
Mediated
Minimized
Modeled
Modified
Monitored
Motivated
Moved
Negotiated
Nominated
Observed
Obtained
Offered
Operated
Optimized
Orchestrated
Ordered
Organized
Originated
Overcame
Oversaw

Participated
Perceived
Performed
Persuaded
Piloted
Pioneered
Placed
Planned
Played
Predicted
Prepared
Prescribed
Presented
Prevented
Printed
Processed
Procured
Produced
Programmed
Projected
Promoted
Proposed
Protected
Proved
Provided
Publicized
Published
Purchased
Quadrupled
Quantified
Questioned
Raised
Ratified
Received
Recognized
Recommended
Reconciled
Recorded
Recruited
Rectified
Redesigned
Reduced
Reevaluated
Referred
Refined

Registered
Regulated
Rehabilitated
Reinforced
Reinformed
Related
Rendered
Reorganized
Reported
Researched
Resolved
Responded
Revamped
Reviewed
Revised
Revitalized
Revived
Scheduled
Screened
Secured
Selected
Separated
Served
Serviced
Set (up)
Shaped
Shifted
Simplified
Sold
Solidified
Solved
Sorted
Sparked
Spearheaded
Specified
Spoke
Staffed
Standardized
Started
Stimulated
Streamlined
Strengthened
Stressed
Stretched
Structured

Studied
Submitted
Substituted
Succeeded
Summarized
Superseded
Supervised
Supplied
Supported
Sustained
Synthesized
Systematized
Taught
Tempered
Temporized
Terminated
Tested
Traced
Tracked
Traded
Trained
Transferred
Transformed
Translated
Treated
Tripled
Trimmed
Turned around
Uncovered
Unified
United
Unraveled
Updated
Utilized
Vacated
Validated
Verified
Widened
Withdrew
Won
Worked
Wrote
Yielded

■ Skills Identification

Skills tend to fall into one of two categories—abstract and concrete. Abstract skills hint at your overall potential; concrete skills are more specifically defined and serve to enhance your credibility. In your résumé, you should list some of each type of skill. Some examples of abstract skills are the ability to organize, quick proficiency at new tasks, and a positive attitude toward work. Some concrete skills are the ability to take dictation, knowledge of computer spreadsheets, and a typing speed of sixty words per minute.

EXERCISE

Make a list of your abstract skills. Then, next to each skill, give a specific example that illustrates your mastery of that skill.

Abstract Skills	**Specific Examples**
Examples: Good organizational skills	Organized a bake sale at my college
Good at managing money	Served as treasurer of college chess club my junior and senior years

Abstract Skills	**Specific Examples**
1.	
2.	
3.	
4.	
5.	

Now make a list of all your concrete skills, such as your familiarity with computer programs and other specific talents you've developed and specialties you've acquired.

Concrete Skills

1. _____
2. _____
3. _____
4. _____
5. _____

Review your lists of abstract and concrete skills. Place check marks by the ones you think are worth including in your résumé. Refer back to this page when you write your résumé.

For more exercises to help make writing your résumé easier, go to Resumania, at www.umn.edu/ohr/ecep/resume.

Types of Résumés

As you assemble your résumé, you'll need to decide which of the two formats below best highlights your strong points. Each type of résumé is good in certain situations, and both are equally acceptable, although the chronological résumé is more common.

■ The Chronological Résumé

This type of résumé highlights the sequence of jobs the applicant has held. The "Experience" section lists jobs in order of dates, giving the most recent position first. After you've listed each employer, city, state, and job title, write a brief job description using strong action words. You may place the dates in the left margin or after each job description, depending on how much you want to highlight them. Be sure you present dates consistently throughout your résumé, such as "5/96–present" or "May 1996–present" or "1994–present." A chronological résumé is best for those who

- have clearly progressed toward their job objective. For example, this format would highlight a job hunter's progression from a clerical, to a supervisory, and then to an upper managerial position because the job titles and the dates of employment would be clearly listed down the left side of the résumé.

- have had no gaps in their job history and want to stress the fact that they have been consistently employed.

■ The Functional Résumé

This type of résumé stresses skills, not dates. After a clear job objective at the top of the résumé, the next heading listed is "Skills." Three or four broad skill areas are identified, each of which should relate to the job objective. For example, if your job objective states, "Seeking a position as an office manager," you might decide to create categories such as "Office Skills," "Managerial Skills," and "Organizational Skills." In each category you could describe how you demonstrated those skills in previous jobs. You would have to draw on your experience from all the positions you've held, both paid and unpaid. A functional résumé is best for those who

- have held a variety of unrelated jobs. For example, if you have worked in a shoe store and a fast-food restaurant, a functional résumé would allow you to stress the fact that you've had experience waiting on customers, regardless of the setting.

- have gaps in their job history. Dates of employment are still listed on the page, but later; they are not the first thing an employer sees.

Look carefully at the sample résumés shown on the following pages. What do you notice first? How have these job hunters magnified their assets and downplayed their weak points? Does one format appeal to you more? Examine each résumé to see which format, chronological or functional, and which layout is best for you. Then it's time to begin preparing a first draft of your own résumé.

Marilyn L. Camire

65 Longwell Road
West Hartford, Connecticut 06119
(203) 555-2642

OBJECTIVE

Position in technically oriented writing or editing.

SKILLS

Excellent writing skills.
Keyboard 70 words per minute.
Thorough knowledge of WordPerfect, MSWord, Excel, PageMaker.

EDUCATION

B.S., Journalism/Technical Writing, expected May 2004. Dixon College, Hartford, Connecticut.

Relevant Course Work: Advanced Technical Writing, Magazine Writing, Copy Editing, Technological Reports I and II, Desktop Publishing, Introduction to Computers.

EXPERIENCE

1999–
present

Publications Assistant, Alumni Office, University of Connecticut (part-time). Produce bimonthly media reports; write copy and take photographs for faculty and alumni newsletters.

1998
Summer

Marketing Assistant (intern), NEC Engineers, Inc., Woodbridge, Connecticut. Wrote sections of proposals; copyedited manuals, brochures, and correspondence.

1997
Summer

Office Assistant, Department of Humanities, Dixon College, Hartford, Connecticut. Prepared mailings, updated computer records, assisted students with registration, performed general office tasks.

ACTIVITIES/INTERESTS

Editor, *Dixon News,* school newspaper, 2000–2001, Assistant Editor, 1999–2000; Copyeditor, 1997.

Secretary, Alpha Phi International Sorority.

References available upon request.

Sample 1: Chronological Résumé

JOSEPH BLACK

PERMANENT ADDRESS
(after 5/30/00)
21 Foxrun Drive
Bayville, Vermont 68725
(513) 555-0932

TEMPORARY ADDRESS
(until 5/30/00)
Barnesville College
212 Metcalf Hall
Barnesville, Vermont 68711
(413) 555-3387

CAREER OBJECTIVE

Seeking employment as an officer in an urban police department.

EDUCATION

A.S., Criminal Justice (to be awarded May 2000), Barnesville College, Barnesville, Vermont. Dean's List, 1998, 1999. Degree also includes courses in Human Relations, Contemporary Social Problems, Report Writing, and Spanish for Law Enforcement.

Bayville Technical College, Bayville, Vermont, 1995.

EMPLOYMENT EXPERIENCE

1998	Barnesville College, Barnesville, Vermont. CAMPUS SECURITY ASSISTANT. Assisted Coordinator of Security with patrolling hallways, admitting visitors, and reporting incidents in residence halls.
1997	Parker's Photography Studio, Kearsage, Vermont. PHOTOGRAPHER. Photographed family portraits and weddings. Assisted customers choosing from proofs. Worked in darkroom. Closed and secured studio.
1996	Smith's Burger Cottage, Barnesville, Vermont. COUNTERPERSON. Responsible for cash drawer averaging $2,000 daily. Took customer orders and delivered food.

PROFESSIONAL AFFILIATIONS

1998–present	Treasurer, New England Association for Students of Criminal Justice.

REFERENCES

References to be furnished upon request.

Sample 2: Chronological Résumé

R. EDUARDO FONÇERAS
15 Spears Street
Peterboro, PA 55162
(504) 555-9071

JOB TARGET
Seeking entry-level employment at a large hotel where I can utilize my computer and customer service skills.

SPECIAL SKILLS/COMPUTER SKILLS
Fluent in written and spoken Spanish. Knowledge of hotel computer software systems.

EDUCATION
Fillmore Community College, Falls, PA.
A.S, Hotel Restaurant Management, expected 2002

Important Courses: Front Office Procedure, Hotel Computer Systems, Hospitality Security Management.

EXPERIENCE AND SKILLS
Mile-away Motel, Falls, PA. *Desk Clerk.* Registered and checked out guests. Trained three new employees. Took reservations and processed payments. Assisted guests with questions and information about local sights. 2000–present.

Krystal Kleen Dry Kleening, Wenster, PA. *Clerk.* Assisted customers with problems and questions. Processed orders. Completed special-order forms. Operated cash register. 1998–1999.

RELATED INTERESTS AND ACTIVITIES
Member, Fillmore Community College Hospitality Club, 2000.

Certified by the American Hotel and Motel Association Educational Institute, 2000.

REFERENCES
Available upon request.

Sample 3: Chronological Résumé

Clarisse Poplar

574 Highland St., #3B, Bolton, TX 87630
(304) 555-4671

Career Objective

Executive secretarial position in a growing corporation.

Summary of Skills

- Proficient in WordPerfect and MSWord
- Experience with various spreadsheet and database programs
- Type 75 words per minute
- Thorough knowledge of all office equipment, including fax machines, postage machines, photocopiers, and switchboards

Education

Coleboro Secretarial School, Coleboro, TX. Executive secretarial major. 2000–2001.

ITX Industries, Brightfield, TX. Completed 15 hours of in-house training in areas of Customer Service, Computers in Business, and Telephone Techniques. 1998.

Experience

ADMINISTRATIVE ASSISTANT (Internship). Bruce M. MacDormand, M.D. Singeburgh, TX. Assisted physician with typing and mailing correspondence, newsletters, invoices, insurance forms. Answered patient questions and assisted receptionist with appointments and telephones. 2001.

RECEPTIONIST. ITX Industries, Brightfield, TX. Greeted clients. Answered phones. Completed light typing and filing. Assisted office staff with mailings and projects. Participated as an assistant and as a student in in-house training sessions. 1996–1998.

DAY CARE AIDE. Little Rainbows Day Care. Bellavista, FL. Conferred with parents. Planned and supervised daily activities and field trips. Assisted with meals. 1996.

References

Available upon request.

Sample 4: Chronological Résumé

Zoë R. Kateman

337 Shasta Ave. • Rainham, IL 60649 • (208) 555-3820 • ZKateman@tec.IL.us

OBJECTIVE

To secure a position as an airline ticket reservationist at a busy metropolitan airport.

EDUCATION

A.S., Travel and Tourism, Illinois Community Technical College, Rainham, IL. Degree to be awarded May 2003. Completed courses in Domestic Travel Procedures (includes SABRE and Worldspan training), PC Applications, and Conversational Spanish.

EXPERIENCE

Office Assistant (Intern). Runaway Travel, Otis, IL. Assisted agents with arranging and booking foreign and domestic travel arrangements. Special assistant for Medco, Inc., travel accounts, serving all 4,000 Medco employees, including management and CEO. Greeted customers. Responded to telephone inquiries. 2000–2001.

Customer Service Representative. Spenser Gifts and Novelties, Charlestown, IL. Assisted customers with selection and purchase of merchandise. Handled cash. Maintained appearance of all store displays. 1996–1998.

EXTRACURRICULAR

Vice President, Illinois Community Technical College Travel Club. Arranged club tours to Orlando and Niagara Falls. Responsible for publicity and financial arrangements for both trips. 2001.

REFERENCES

Available upon request.

Sample 5: Chronological Résumé

Michelle Lee

2421 Sheehan Circle
St. George, OR
(304) 555-1610
MLee@juneau.com

GOAL
Seeking employment as a CAD Manager.

EMPLOYMENT

CAD Operator. Drawings Unlimited, Holiday, OR. Experience with AutoCAD R13, Data-CAD 7, and MiniCAD 6. Assisted with client conferences. Trained three new hires. Voted Employee of the Year for 1999. 1997–present.

CAD Operator. David White Associates, St. George, OR. Assisted designers with residential planning, layout, and structural calculations. Produced drawings both manually and electronically. 1996.

EDUCATION

A.S., Yeaton Technical College, Asbestos, WA. 2000. Graduated Magna Cum Laude. Important Courses: Computer Information Systems, Design Drafting I and II, Technical Writing.

REFERENCES
Available upon request.

Sample 6: Chronological Résumé

Leon Kensington
75 Curtis Lane
Tilton, NH 03276
(603) 555-3640

OBJECTIVE

Management trainee position in retail sales, using skills in design, administration, and public contact.

PROFESSIONAL EXPERIENCE AND SKILLS

Management
Coordinated operations, managed and assisted in sales at Peterson Stationery.

Managed small medical laboratory at Petrie Laboratories.

Trained military personnel in hazardous-waste procedures at Pease Air Force Base.

Administration
Wrote and catalogued procedures for medical laboratory in Bow, NH. Designed new record forms, evaluated and carried out daily work priorities.

Coordinated numerous experiments from inception through subsequent interpretation and reporting of findings.

Technical Skills
Type 75 wpm. Familiar with most desktop publishing and spreadsheet programs.

WORK HISTORY

2000	Research Assistant—Petrie Laboratories, Bow, NH.
1998	Sales & Operations—Peterson Stationery, Concord, NH.
1996–1998	Hotline Volunteer—Women's Crisis Center, Generra, MA.
1986–1996	Family management and independent study.

EDUCATION

B.S., Retailing, Metropolitan College, Providence, RI.

References available on request.

Sample 7: Functional Résumé

Carl Fortier

778 Sterling Park Road
Natick, MA 02134
(508) 555-9898

JOB OBJECTIVE

Bank teller in a large metropolitan bank.

SKILLS AND EXPERIENCE

Customer Service   Handled customer inquiries and complaints at brokerage firm. Educated and advised customers on new insurance products.

Sales   Solicited donations for renovations of community gardens.

Secretarial   Type 75 words per minute.
Experienced data entry clerk.
Recently completed coursework in Business Computer Applications.

EMPLOYMENT HISTORY

Insurance Agent	Whittemore Insurance, Natick, MA	2000
Office Assistant	Johnson Brokerage Firm, Stow, MA	1998
Medical Assistant	Sam Donagan, M.D., Gloucester, MA	1996–1998
Assistant Teacher	Wee Ones Day Care, Hyannis, MA	1995

EDUCATION

A.S., Business Studies, Merritt College, Boston, MA	2001
Certificate & License, Medical Assisting, City College, Boston, MA	1996

References available upon request.

Sample 8: Functional Résumé

Jefferson M. Sidney

4 Maple Street
Vernon, CO
(703) 555-0074

JOB OBJECTIVE: Day Care Center Assistant Manager

SKILLS

Curriculum Development: Planned curriculum units on Native American Studies, Forest Studies, and Dinosaurs for children aged 3–5 as part of practicum experience.
Wrote three children's books (unpublished) as part of Children's Literature course.

Art/Creativity: Planned, coordinated, and participated in creation of a full wall mural at Greater Vernon Boys' Club.
Experienced in introducing manipulatives, paints, beads, and cooking to children aged 2–5.

Conferencing: Observed children in Kid's Inn preschool center and prepared weekly observation reports to be shared with classmates and site supervisor. Discussed feeding and toileting behaviors with parents of two young children under my supervision.

EDUCATION

Barlow Community College, Boynton, CO. A.S., Early Childhood Education, 2002. Coursework included:

Creative Development	Exceptional and At-Risk Children
Day Care Organization	Children's Literature

Completed 120 hours of observation and 150 hours of practical training.

WORK HISTORY

Counselor, Greater Vernon Boys' Club, Vernon, CO, 2000–present
Day Care Aide (practicum), Wunderkind Day Care, Clayton, CO, 2000
Deli Clerk, Shop 'N' Save, Vernon, CO, 1999
Child Care Provider, Ms. Mitzu Park, Vernon, CO, 1999

RELATED INTERESTS

Big Brother, Big Brothers of America, Inc., 1999–present

REFERENCES

Available upon request.

Sample 9: Functional Résumé

EXERCISE
Résumé Revision

The résumé on the following page contains at least a dozen errors. Look it over and begin planning some corrections.

This résumé is clearly a first draft, and it will need many revisions before it is ready to be presented to an employer. In its current condition, this résumé makes a negative statement about the candidate.

Try your own revision of this résumé. Practice with both chronological and functional formats and experiment with your layout. See what a difference you can make in Vicki's chances of getting an interview; then compare your revisions with the two other versions that follow here. (Please note that you may have to be creative and fill in some of the details omitted in the original version.)

RESUME   3/28/00

Vicki Bahtsas
rfd2 box 199
Red Rock, Arizona

Personnel Data
Separated, 2 children
Excellant Health

EDUCATION

Red Rock H.S. 1996–98
GED '97
Attempted 5 courses at Mesa Comm. College

Experience

Schuylers' Dept. Store, 491 Los Nubes Blvd.Autusville, Arizona
(415) 555-6130
January–Nov. 1993

Part-time Assembly Line worker at Microtex Incorp. Carille, AZ 16 Industrial Drive 8/93–
now I make printed circuit boards and do many p-50 forms I also help QC when needed.

HOBBIES

Painting, voleyball, suntanning, biking, poetry, basketball, and all sports, reading, guitar, etc.
also a singer in the choir of Faith Christian Church.

Sample 10: Poorly Done Résumé

Did you notice the misspellings, sloppy format, and lack of information about skills? Pertinent information is omitted, while irrelevant data is readily apparent. The applicant's name is not especially noticeable, and there is no phone number or mention of references. The date at the top of the page is unnecessary. Also note the inconsistencies in the presentation of dates and order of information.

By now you may realize how much work is involved in résumé revision. Although Vicki's first draft has many errors, it is not unusually bad for a first attempt. The act of "diving in" and committing information takes courage and, at the very least, provides a place to start.

After you've drafted one revision of this résumé, compare your work with another person's draft. Do you agree with your classmate's revisions? What further changes could be made?

VICKI BAHTSAS

RFD 2, Box 199
Red Rock, AZ 66114
(415) 555-0938

Job Objective:	Position as a Medical Secretary in a busy pediatric practice.

Experience:

1999–present	*Child Care Provider.* Self-employed, Red Rock, AZ. Care for three children aged six months to five years. Plan and supervise activities and meals. Confer with parents.
1998	*Medical Secretary* (Externship). Red Rock Pediatric Group, Red Rock, AZ. Assisted receptionist with greeting patients. Processed various health insurance forms. Filed and retrieved medical records. Assisted with transcription of physicians' notes.
1995	*Assembler* (part-time). Microtex, Inc., Carille, AZ. Assembled printed circuit boards. Cross-trained to assist quality control staff. Completed daily production reports.
1993–1995	*Sales Associate.* Schuyler's Department Store, Autusville, AZ. Assisted customers with purchases and returns. Trained three junior associates. Operated cash register. Managed cosmetics department in manager's absence.

Education:

2000	Mesa Community College, Mesa, AZ. Medical Secretary/Transcriptionist Diploma Program.
	Relevant Courses: Medical Terminology, Medical Machine Transcription, Word/Information Processing, Office Systems Management.

References:

References provided on request.

Sample 11: Revised Résumé in Chronological Format

VICKI BAHTSAS

RFD 2, Box 199
Red Rock, AZ 66114
(415) 555-0938

Objective:

Position as a medical secretary in a busy pediatric practice.

Skills:

- Secretarial—Type 60 wpm. Experienced medical transcriptionist and receptionist. Processed insurance forms. Filed and retrieved medical records.
- Computer Skills—Knowledge of AppointmentBook software as well as various spreadsheet and word-processing programs.
- Public Contact—Assisted department store customers with purchases and returns. Confer with parents of young children on progress and behaviors.
- Teamwork—Worked closely with seven other employees on circuit board assembly line. Cross-trained to assist with quality control staff. Assisted store manager with cosmetics department in department manager's absence.

Education:

Mesa Community College, Mesa, AZ. Diploma, Medical Secretary/ Transcriptionist. 2000.

Relevant Courses: Medical Terminology. Medical Machine Transcription. Word/Information Processing. Office Systems Management.

Work History:

Child Care Provider, self-employed. Red Rock, AZ. 1999–present

Medical Secretary (Externship), Red Rock Pediatric Group, Red Rock, AZ. 1998.

Assembler (part-time), Microtex, Inc., Carille, AZ. 1995.

Sales Associate, Schuyler's Department Store, Autusville, AZ. 1993–1995.

References:

References provided on request.

Sample 12: Revised Résumé in Functional Format

EXERCISE
Résumé Worksheet

This worksheet is the place for brainstorming. By completing it you will be sure to remember all your education, skills, and experience, and you will be better able to organize your thoughts. Thinking through your skills should prove helpful not only for writing your résumé but also during the interview process.

As in any brainstorming exercise, there are no wrong answers; include everything you can think of under each category. It is best to complete items two through eleven only after you've let the information in item one sit for a few days. This way you'll be able to gain some distance from your work and your revisions will be more effective.

Before beginning, you may want to photocopy the résumé worksheet for future use as your career progresses.

1. Fill in the information requested in the six following sections.

    a. Job Objective

        Career fields in which you'd be interested _____

        Specific positions or types of positions _____

        Skills you'd like to use _____

    b. Education Remember to list schooling in reverse chronological order (most recent first).

        College attended (name) _____ (city/state) _____

        Degree received/date _____

        Relevant or important courses _____

        Other college attended (name) _____ (city/state) _____

        Degree received/date _____

        Relevant or important courses _____

        Additional educational training (seminars, workshops, extracurricular activities) _____

c. **Experience** As above, list experience in reverse chronological order. Include volunteer work and internships (list in parentheses after job title). You may need additional sheets to fully describe your skills.

Employer (City/State)	Job Title/ Dates Worked	Description of Skills (Use Action Verbs)

d. **Awards and Honors**

Award/Honor	Date Received

e. **Professional Affiliations**

Organization	Year Joined	Position Held

f. **Interests and Activities** List all extracurricular activities, interests, hobbies, volunteer work, clubs to which you belong, etc.

_____

_____

_____

2. Referring back to item 1(c), revise your job duties here. Reorder your skills so that the most impressive appear first in the job description. Use strong verbs to begin each sentence.

Position 1 _____

Description of skills _____

Position 2 _____

Description of skills _____

Position 3 _____

Description of skills _____

3. Using the ideas generated in item 1(a), write several one-sentence versions of your job objective here. Then circle the one that is most clear and concise.

    a. _____

    b. _____

    c. _____

4. Review the previous sections. Cross out any mention of controversial, political, or religious activities.

5. Using the space to the left of each heading in item 1, number the headings in the order in which you'd like them to appear on your résumé. Remember, place your strongest sections close to the top of the page. If you have a strong career objective, it should appear second only to your name and address. References are usually stated last. The order of the rest of these elements is flexible. Mark an *X* by any sections you would not like to include.

DIVE IN

6. Now try a draft of your résumé. Lay out the rough information you have here. Where will the headings be placed? How will you present the employment information? Where will you use capital letters, bold print, italics, white space, or underlining? By now you should have a rough draft of your résumé.

7. Show your draft to at least one other person who has had experience working with résumés. A teacher, employer, or businessperson would be ideal. Have a brief conversation with him or her.

    a. What does the person notice first? Is this what you had intended to highlight?

    b. Is your career objective clear? Is it too vague or too narrow?

    c. Are all your strengths included?

    d. Are the descriptions of your skills thorough, and do they start with action verbs?

    e. Is the layout neat and eye-catching?

    f. What other comments does this person have about your résumé? Would the person hire you?

8. Proofread carefully. Be sure there are no typos or misspellings. Make sure you have handled dates and punctuation in a consistent style.

9. Print your résumé on a piece of plain white paper.

10. Proofread again.

11. Using the copy on white paper as a master, photocopy your résumé on good quality paper, sold in office supply stores and print shops. You may also consider having your résumé printed. Although this is an added expense, it will help to make your résumé look more professional.

What to Do About Gaps in Your Job History

For a variety of reasons, many people have unexplained gaps in their job histories. Some were not employed outside the home after they had children; some may have taken time off for travel, medical reasons, or soul-searching. People who are reentering the job market after retiring or after a long job search may also wonder how to express this time appropriately on a résumé.

If you are concerned about how to explain the gaps in your job history, consider the following suggestions:

- **Create a functional résumé.** Emphasize your objective; then list three or four transferable skill areas. Describe all the ways in which you have demonstrated those skills. Place the dates of your employment in a section lower on the page.

- **Write a chronological résumé.** Place the dates of your employment at the *end* of each job description.

- **Minimize the gap.** Give only the years of employment instead of the month and the year.

- **Create a job title to explain the time gap.** Many people actually have done productive, albeit unpaid, work during their "gap time." Be honest but creative. Could you call yourself an independent consultant? Family manager? One woman who spent years entertaining her husband's international business clients for weeks at a time decided on a title of International Hostess/Party Planner. Be sure not to overlook volunteer work or internships. Create a job title and put the word *volunteer* or *intern* in parentheses following the title.

- **Create new headings on your résumé.** If your work experience is limited or spotty, stress other strengths. Create categories for "Special Skills," "Awards and Honors," "Interests and Activities," "Relevant Courses," or "Additional Training."

KEY POINT

- **Don't lie.** In the interview, explain any time gaps briefly but honestly. Remember, even a great résumé does not get you the job. *You* get yourself the job during the interview. In minimizing time gaps in your résumé, your intention is not to deceive the employer but to prevent yourself from being eliminated before the interview. Plan ahead about how to explain the time gap should the question arise.

Résumé Alternatives

While the chronological and functional résumés are the most common formats for presenting one's experience, they are not the only options. Using an alternative format can help you stand out in a crowd. It can also be seen as a fresh way to organize information that transcends job descriptions and dates of employment.

Sometimes an alternative résumé can be used in conjunction with your traditional résumé. You'll have to decide what is most appropriate for you in your individual situation. Here are some résumé alternatives to consider:

Narrative résumés These are conversational in tone, telling a story about the candidate's career progression while integrating relevant personal data. Stick to one page, breaking up long blocks of text with headlines and subheads. You may also want to use bullets to present information. The narrative résumé may be combined with a letter starting with a personal greeting, such as "Dear Ms. Smith: I am pleased to send you further information about my work experience, as you requested."

Biographies Create a concise, interesting story about your background and most impressive accomplishments. Keep your summary to about five or six paragraphs. Lay out the information on a single page, using an easy-to-read type style, and possibly some graphic elements, like a border or even a head-and-shoulders photo of yourself.

Addenda An addendum is a single page that accompanies your résumé and describes a particular skill or position in more detail. It gives you the opportunity to elaborate on your most impressive or relevant experience. Good topics for an addendum include: key volunteer, internship or life experiences; computer skills, including hardware, software, and networking systems used; training experiences, including classes taught or attended; project leadership, including the number of staff, budget, and goals accomplished.

Job-search business cards If your job hunt is well targeted, the key points of the search will fit on a business card printed on one or both sides, or in a fold-over tent format. These points would include one to three areas of expertise, your job-search goal, and your name and contact information. Distribute your business cards at networking meetings, social events, business open houses, job fairs, and interviews.

Work samples If you have been previously employed or have taken courses directly related to the job for which you're applying, you may consider sending actual examples of your work. These samples should be truly reflective of the quality of work you do. They should be accompanied by an explanatory cover letter and/or a traditional résumé. Keep in mind that your work samples may not be returned to you, so you may want to send only photocopies.

Résumé Software

One of the job-hunting tools you might want to consider adding to your repertoire is a résumé software package. Although some packages tend to be a bit simplistic and generic in terms of the types of résumés they create, they can certainly serve as a good starting point.

Most packages offer you the option of creating either a functional or chronological résumé. You'll probably be able to choose from several different templates of each. Depending on the sophistication of the package, you'll have varying degrees of flexibility from there. Some packages will offer you choices of fonts, graphic elements, colors, and layouts. Many are actually glorified word-processing programs. Just make sure that the package you choose gives you clear, step-by-step instructions for inputting your information.

Probably the best reason for investing in résumé software is if you intend to customize your résumé for different employers. Some software will simplify that task while creating crisp, professional layouts.

You can purchase résumé software packages at any office supply or computer store. Packages cost from $20 to $75, depending on their capabilities. Read the boxes carefully and decide whether you need all the bells and whistles.

KEY POINT

The important thing to remember is that résumé software is not a substitute for your creative thinking and your knowledge of the job market for your field. To create an effective résumé, you, and only you, must take the time to determine how to present your skills and experience in the best light for the type of position you seek. Customize your résumé and be sure to continue to follow all the basic résumé do's and don'ts. Take extra care to ensure that the final layout is pleasing and not too "busy."

Make Your Résumé Computer Friendly

In today's highly automated work environment, many companies turn to computers to store résumés, cover letters, and job applications. Using résumé scanning software and automated applicant tracking systems, companies can easily file and retrieve applicant information. Many companies also use on-line databases to locate applicants. For these reasons, it makes good sense to have a scannable version of your résumé and cover letter. This applies even if you only send them to selected employers you know are using automated systems or use them to put information on the Internet. Following a few simple guidelines will help ensure that your data is accurately scanned.

1. **Send originals.** Photocopies or faxed copies often lack clarity and are difficult to scan. If you must send a fax for the purpose of speed, mention in your cover sheet that originals are on their way by mail.

2. **Choose white or off-white paper.** Text printed on colored paper lacks contrast and is harder to read. Very few computers have the ability to read text with low contrast. Use only black ink for the same reason.

3. **Use 8½″ × 11″ paper printed on one side.** Many scanners can't handle larger sizes. Information printed on a second side may be missed or can make both sides harder to read by a scanner.

4. **Select easy-to-read sans serif fonts.** Avoid fancy type styles. Stick with popular styles such as Helvetica or Arial in point sizes of 10 to 14. Don't compress any lines of text. Don't print your résumé using a dot-matrix printer or a worn printer cartridge.

5. **No scripts, italics, underlining, or boldface text.** These features can destroy text clarity since characters can run together. Even though most of the newer software programs can read them, you have no way of knowing what your prospective employer uses. Eliminate these features from your résumé by copying the file you used to create your printed version and removing the format commands.

6. **Avoid horizontal and vertical lines.** Any extra lines can be misread. Sometimes vertical lines are read as the letter *I*.

7. **Use wide margins around the text, at least 1″.** Text inside the margins may be missed.

8. **Avoid graphics.** Any information placed within a graphic can be lost. Steer clear of boxes and shading as well.

9. **Skip hollow bullets.** If you list information with bullets, use solid dots instead of hollow ones. Computers will read hollow dots as the letter *o*.

10. **Use parentheses around telephone numbers.** Place the area code of your telephone number within parentheses, as opposed to offsetting it with a hyphen or slash. Because parentheses are how a computer identifies a phone number, avoid using parentheses anywhere else in the document.

11. **Separate your e-mail address, phone number, and fax number.** List your e-mail address, phone number, and fax number on different lines to avoid the chance of a scanner running them together.

12. **No folds, no staples.** Send your letter in a full-size 9″ × 12″ envelope to avoid creases from folding. Use a paper clip to attach pages, since staples would have to be removed before the pages could be fed into the scanner. Folds and holes impair the scanning software's ability to read the document.

Be sure to put your name and a page number at the top of each page in case the pages separate.

For more information on making your résumé computer friendly, go to Creating your Résumé by Resumix at www.resumix.com/resume/resumeindex.html.

■ Using Keywords

When résumés and cover letters are scanned or downloaded, the data from them are placed into a database for retrieval when a need arises. Employers and recruiters search résumé databases using keywords, which are nouns and phrases that highlight areas of expertise, industry-related jargon, achievements, and other distinctive features of an applicant's work history.

Wording your résumé for the computer means that verbs, the hallmark of a good paper résumé, are less useful than nouns because recruiters more often search for nouns. You should even consider the form of the nouns you're using. *Management,* for example, can be dangerous because it would be missed by a recruiter who typed in *manager.* Your best bet is to put down both words. You may even want to have a section called "Keywords" that unabashedly plays to the computer, seeking to pop up in as many employer searches as possible.

KEY POINT

The job seeker with the most keywords, plus required experience, rises to the top of the candidate heap. Cover your bases by lacing your résumé and cover letter with career-specific keywords.

Choosing the best keywords is largely dependent on your career objective and the type of position you're hoping to obtain. For example, here is a brief list of some keywords that could help a candidate for a teaching position land on an employer's "hit list":

- Private and public school
- Special education
- Master's degree
- Guidance counselor
- Detail oriented
- School board
- Extracurricular activities
- Gifted students
- Inner-city schools
- Teacher-of-the-year award
- Budget planning
- Textbook author

- Computer literate
- Windows 98, Microsoft Office
- Spreadsheet development

EXERCISE

Review your résumé. Make a list of keywords you've used. Then look for opportunities to insert additional keywords. Revise your résumé accordingly.

■ Posting Your Résumé

Now that you've created a scannable version of your résumé, you're ready to post it on the Internet. Posting sites and services offer different ways for employers to access their résumé databases. Some allow employers and even job candidates direct access. Others require that employers tell the service what kind of job they want to fill and what qualifications they seek. The database service then searches the database and provides the employer with résumés from suitable applicants. When deciding whether to post your résumé, be sure to ask the following questions:

- Does the database post the kinds of jobs that interest you?
- Would your ideal employer by likely to search this database?
- How long does a résumé stay on the system?
- What are the posting requirements?
- Are there any costs associated with posting?
- Can access to your résumé be restricted in any way, such as to avoid having your current employer see it?

Strategic posting and routine monitoring are the best ways to increase your likelihood of job-hunting success and to ensure that your résumé doesn't float aimlessly all over the Internet.

Targeting
Potential Employers

Generate Job Leads

Often the most difficult aspect of finding a new job is lining up interviews. Many job hunters make the mistake of relying exclusively on help wanted ads. They're missing some important ways to help generate leads. Here, then, are some ideas for improving your chances of landing a job interview:

DIVE IN

1. **Personal contacts.** It has often been said, "It's not what you know, but who you know." The reality is that most people get jobs through personal contacts, also called networking. You should get in touch with your friends, former work associates, suppliers, vendors, bankers, doctors, neighbors, old college friends, fellow professionals, organization members, and anyone else you can think of to see if they can offer any job leads. Also, don't forget to ask them for the names of any of their own contacts who might be able to help you in your job-search networking.

2. **Informational interviews.** Perfect for the person just out of college or for those seeking a career or geographic change, these interviews allow you to gather information that may prove useful in your job search. Choose someone in the company to speak with about his or her occupation: what it takes to be successful, where the best-paying jobs can be found, how to break into the field, and so forth. You should also ask the person you meet with to recommend anyone else who might be willing to talk with you.

3. **Managers who just got promoted.** You can find the names of these people in the Promotions section of the newspaper. They may be building new staffs.

4. **Calls to potential employers.** Sometimes it's worth the risk of rejection to call employers directly and explain why you'd like to work for them and why you think you're qualified for a position.

5. **A fax or e-mail.** If a particular job you're interested in calls for aggressiveness, try sending a fax or e-mail in response to the ad.

6. **Growth companies.** Growth companies (listed under "Growth Firms" in the *Business Periodicals Index*) are continually hiring new people.

7. **Newsletter editors.** Most industries have newsletters or trade journals. The editors of these publications are often aware of jobs in the market.

8. **Venture capital companies.** People in these firms are frequently aware of businesses that are hiring, particularly for high-level jobs.

9. **A position wanted ad.** Many newspapers and trade publications have a special section for advertising the position you're seeking. Briefly state your accomplishments and experience.

10. **Employment agencies.** Call employment agencies in your area and see which ones tend to have positions for people in your field. Fortunately, it is most often the employer who pays the agency a fee once you've been placed.

11. **Executive search firms.** Contact these firms if you're seeking a management position paying a salary over $45,000. You should write a letter that describes your job requirements, lists your salary needs, and details your experience.

12. **Job services.** Most state job services have a professional employee placement division.

13. **Alumni placement offices.** Keep in touch with your college placement offices even if it's been a while since you graduated. They often hear of jobs that require a little more experience than that of the average graduating senior.

14. **Trade/professional organizations.** Join these associations to begin networking with people in your field. This is a great way to make contacts.

15. **Check the Internet.** Many companies use the World Wide Web to list their job openings. In addition to individual companies' listings, there are literally thousands of classified ads on the web. See Chapter 6 for more about job hunting on-line.

16. **Use the Yellow Pages.** Even the phone book can yield leads. Let your fingers do the walking, then start dialing.

Finding a job is often a numbers game. The key to winning is to have as many irons in the fire as possible. If you're participating in all these activities, you're more likely to find that perfect job sooner. The rest of this section gives you some tips on following through with the first two important items above, networking and informational interviews.

■ Networking Chart

KEY POINT

A large percentage of job hunters find jobs not through classified ads or placement services but through personal contacts. Ask around. You'll find that most people learn of job openings through a relative, friend, or friend of a friend. Initially you may feel uncomfortable asking others for help in locating employment, but remember that most people are flattered to be considered a resource. Making the series of contacts necessary to find the ideal position isn't easy. You need to be friendly, persistent in your search, and sure of the type of job you seek.

Begin by completing the left-hand tier of the chart on page 61. (You may want to photocopy this chart for future use.) Tell as many people as you can about the type of career that you're seeking. If necessary, fill them in on your background and skills. Ask if they know of anyone who might be interviewing or of anyone else that you should contact. As you learn of more people who could help you, add their names on the appropriate lines. Be sure to thank everyone who provides you with even the tiniest hint.

**Names/Phone Numbers
of Initial Contacts
(friends/family)**   **Names They Provide**   **Names They Provide**

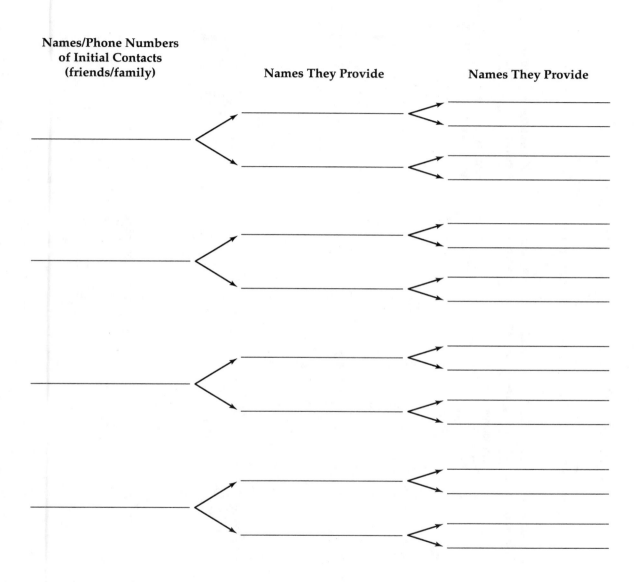

KEEPING TRACK OF YOUR CONTACTS

In generating leads, you'll develop a list of contacts. Photocopy this page for future use. Keep track of your contacts by filling out the chart below. Continue to add to the list as you make additional contacts.

Contact Person Name/Phone Number or E-Mail	Relationship/ Recommended by	Occupation/ Where Employed	Last Date of Contact	Suggested Next Date of Contact	Additional Action Required	Contacts He/ She Provided
Example: Mark Bergen (617) 555-9919	Coworker at last job	Accountant, Hyde Accounting	9/12/97	9/30/97	Send copy of résumé to him	Mary Smith, Telco (617) 555-1234

Turn Dead Ends into Live Contacts

DIVE IN

There will be times when you contact someone (either by phone or in person) who is willing to be helpful but, unfortunately, has no job openings for you. Here's where an assertive approach may work to your benefit. Frankly, if you don't ask, you won't get. So go for it!

When there are no particular job openings within a particular department, use the following questions to help a contact help you:

1. Who else in the company might need someone with my skills and experience?

2. Does your company have any other divisions or subsidiaries that might need someone with my attributes?

3. Do you know anyone in my field who might have a lead for me?

4. Can you suggest any other companies that might need someone with my qualifications?

5. Whom should I speak to there?

6. Do you know anyone at (name of company you're interested in)?

7. When do you anticipate an opening in your company?

8. Are you planning any expansion or new projects that might create an opening?

9. Do you have any part-time or freelance opportunities for me?

As always, be sure to thank your contact people both verbally and in writing for any help they provide.

Read the Classifieds

Classified ads that appear in your local newspaper and in trade journals are an obvious source of job leads. Depending on the position advertised and the state of the economy, a classified ad can receive anywhere from a very small to an overwhelming response. If you answer a classified ad and are a viable candidate, you will most likely be contacted for an interview. Be sure that you have made arrangements to have your phone answered during all working hours, even if only by an answering machine. You always risk being passed up for an interview if the employer can't easily contact you.

There are three kinds of classified ads. *Straight classified ads* run in small type under ten lines and are often categorized by position. *Display ads* are larger and often give more detail about the job's requirements. The *blind ad* indicates no company name, address, or telephone number. You respond by sending your résumé to a box number and have no way of knowing where your materials will eventually end up. Many companies choose to run blind ads so their current employees and competition won't know they plan to add to or replace staff.

Be careful if you notice a blind ad that appears repeatedly. This often means that the company experiences a high turnover rate in that position and does not wish to list its name each time it advertises for a replacement. If you apply to a blind ad and receive no response, not even a polite rejection letter, don't be surprised. Companies that run blind ads often choose to reveal themselves only to candidates they consider hiring.

As you read the classifieds, you will notice that employment agencies regularly run ads to attract qualified candidates for placement. Go ahead and send your résumé along if you are interested in the position, but be sure to notice whether the ad indicates "fee paid" or "no fees." This means that if you obtain a job through the employment agency, your employer will pay the placement fee, not you. If this is not indicated in an ad, be sure to ask the agency. Although paying a fee to obtain the right position is not necessarily bad, you should be aware of the fee and exactly what you'll be receiving for it. A standard fee can range from several weeks' to several months' pay, depending on the agency and the caliber of the position.

KEY POINT

Be especially wary of employment agencies that request an up-front fee. Check out these companies with the Better Business Bureau, ask a lot of questions, and carefully read any contracts you're asked to sign before handing over your cash. Remember, if it sounds too good to be true, it probably is.

EXERCISE

EXERCISE

Find the classified section of your local newspaper, preferably a Sunday edition. If you live in a relatively small town, use the nearest large newspaper. Locate a sample of each type of ad: straight, display, and blind. Also see if you can find an ad for a position in your field. What can you learn from these ads about the salary, job requirements, and employment outlook in your future profession?

■ Finding *All* the Job Ads

KEY POINT

Beyond the Sunday classified ads of a newspaper, there are many other resources to consider. Check out trade and professional publications, association newsletters and web sites, job hotlines, public employment service job banks, electronic bulletin boards, and career sites on the Internet.

It's also a good idea to take the time to look through ads in fields outside your own. You might find a related position or discover that you fit into a new career field.

When it comes time to apply to ads, don't just respond to those that match your skills and interests exactly, but to any openings for which you might be considered, even jobs for which you're slightly overqualified or underqualified. Whereas all employers hope to find a perfect candidate, often they are forced to adjust their expectations to fit the applicant pool.

As you read the classified ads, take note of any companies doing major recruitment. Often, they will advertise only selected openings but may have others available. It might be worth a letter or phone call to the company's human resources department to investigate further.

Don't choose to not respond to an ad just because it uses a box number and does not mention the company's name. Many quality companies use this anonymous method to avoid being inundated with résumés. If the job sounds good, it's worth applying for.

If you see multiple ads from one company for different positions, apply separately to each position that interests you. The exception to this rule would be if you know (usually from a phone call to the human resources department) that the company uses a job computer to track applications. In that case, your résumé would be entered into a database, which is then searched as different positions open. The same advice would apply if you have been rejected by a company. Don't hesitate to reapply if a new position opens up, unless you know that the company uses a job computer for tracking.

Making Contacts at Job Fairs

Too many people, too little time, and too disorganized is how many job seekers view job fairs. But with the right preparation and game plan, the job fair can be a great way to get in the door of companies that you might otherwise never get to know.

Companies participate in job fairs usually for one of two reasons: to fill current positions or to collect résumés for anticipated future openings. Because they must usually spend hundreds or thousands of dollars to participate, their presence alone says they are serious.

If you've never been to a job fair before, here's what to expect. Each participating company will set up a table staffed by representatives. The representatives are there to greet you, tell you something about their company, and, most importantly, assess whether you might be a potential candidate for employment. Companies that have the most urgent need will often rent an interview room in addition to the table space where they can do on-the-spot qualifying of candidates.

INTERNET

To find out when and where job fairs are being held, check with your college career office, keep an eye on your local newspaper, and visit www.jobtrak.com, which maintains a career fair calendar.

To produce the best results from a job fair, consider these tips:

1. **Find out in advance which companies plan to be present.** Often the show's promoters print a list and make it available to the public. Also, ads promoting the job fair often list participants.

2. **Determine which companies are your primary targets.** These are the companies you want to be sure to find at the show. Do a little advance research

A job fair can be a great way to get in the door of companies that you might otherwise be unable to access. (© Steve Rubin/The Image Works)

about them and you'll make a solid impression when you talk to their representatives. Look up the companies on the Internet or at your campus career office, or go to the library to research them in back issues of your local paper, the *Wall Street Journal, Business Week,* or other business publications.

3. **Dress for a job, not a fair.** Conservative, professional attire is the way to go. Look upon the job fair like a job interview, and dress accordingly.

4. **Practice your delivery.** First, go to a few booths of companies that you're not interested in. Use them to hone your presentation and get comfortable in the job fair environment before moving on to your primary targets.

5. **Give yourself enough time to be thorough.** Job fairs may last several hours and some even several days, so you should have plenty of time to accomplish your goals. Take the time to evaluate each company and to meet the representatives of your key targets. At popular companies, you may have to wait in line.

6. **Bring enough résumés to hand out copies liberally.** Bring your résumés in a folder, portfolio cover, or notebook, and don't be embarrassed to pass them out. That's what companies are there for—to collect résumés.

DIVE IN

7. **Be professional when you meet representatives.** Treat your meeting like a brief job interview. Shake hands, state your name, and be prepared to give a two-minute introduction about yourself.

8. **Ask questions.** In addition to giving information about yourself, job fairs are also a great place to get information. In meeting with the representatives, try to learn about their companies and obtain names of contacts to whom you can personally send your résumé. Ask the representatives for business cards so you can reference them in writing cover letters to contacts (i.e., "I met Sarah Jones at a recent job fair, and she suggested I contact you.").

9. **Make notes.** Bring a notebook or write notes on the back of business cards to help you remember useful tidbits of information about the company or representative. Employ that information in writing follow-up thank-you notes or future cover letters to the company.

10. **Collect company material.** At most booths, you'll find a display of corporate literature that you can use to learn about the company—its capabilities, corporate philosophy, and operations.

11. **Shoot for an interview, not a job.** Your goal at a job fair is to obtain a follow-up interview. Rarely do companies hire for professional positions on the spot. Instead, they contact their best applicants within a few weeks (sometimes months) of the job fair and schedule appointments for interviews at their company.

12. **Look, listen, and learn.** Use a job fair to gain insight about employers, practice your interviewing skills, and get a sense of the competition by checking out other job hunters.

Research Companies

KEY POINT

One of the most important steps in job hunting is to research potential employers. The more you know about a company, the more specific you can be in your cover letter and the more direct you can be in your interview. Your research will also help you decide whether a particular company is one with which you'd like to be associated.

The following list describes some ways to research potential employers. Depending on your individual situation, some of these methods will be more appropriate than others.

1. **Check the Internet.** The World Wide Web is a great place to start. It is an excellent tool for researching companies and industries. Most companies today, big and small, have a web site that you can locate using a major search en-

gine or by calling the company directly and asking for its Internet address. Typically, the web site will contain information about the company, its products or services, key personnel, and any newsworthy advances or changes.

2. **Subscribe to your local newspaper.** Keep your eyes open for any stories on the company. Many newspapers also have cataloged archives in which you could find past clippings. You may even be able to access those archives online via the Internet.

3. **Read trade literature.** Most firms regularly distribute information on their new products, services, and employees in business-to-business magazines and industry trade journals.

4. **Learn about the company's competitors.** Call to solicit their sales literature. Use this information to learn not only about the competition but also about the field.

5. **Attend trade shows.** Many companies participate in local and national trade shows relevant to their industry. Visit their booths and ask about their products, markets, achievements, and future plans. This may also be a good way to obtain the names of the appropriate people to contact for employment.

6. **Attend meetings of clubs or trade organizations in your field.** You'll be able to learn about the industry and also about your potential employer. To find out about relevant associations, try the *Encyclopedia of Associations*, available in most large libraries. Some libraries allow you to access this reference publication on-line from your computer. Once you have the association names, you may want to see if they have web sites that can provide you with ideas for additional industry resources and also potential employers and specific contact names.

7. **Purchase the company's product.** If it is not feasible for you to buy the product the company makes, try to locate an individual or a firm that does and ask for input on the company.

8. **Ask suppliers and distributors for information.** They can give you an insight into a company's business practices.

9. **Obtain financial data.** If the company is a public corporation, you can solicit an annual report as a potential investor. This document provides a wealth of information, from sales volume and product distribution to plans for the future. (If the company is privately owned, this information may be difficult to acquire.)

10. **Call the Better Business Bureau.** It might be worth finding out if the company has had any complaints lodged against it.

11. **Visit the local chamber of commerce.** Local chambers often keep information on the businesses in their community. Chamber employees might even

be able to give you some personal insights if they have had an opportunity to interact with the company.

12. **Speak to ex-employees.** If you know someone who has worked for the company in the past, he or she might be able to give you helpful input. Remember to take this information with a grain of salt, since ex-employees' opinions may be based on their reasons for leaving.

13. **Call or visit your local library.** Ask at the reference desk how you would go about researching a particular company. Librarians can often steer you toward a wealth of resources.

14. **Be resourceful.** Try to come up with some of your own ideas or contacts for getting information about a company.

Effective Networking

Good networking is about building relationships. The more people you know, the more connected you will be in your field. And connected people learn about job openings earlier, meet more people at a high level, and generally know more about their industries. Furthermore, connected people are more valuable to their future employers because they keep current on the developments and players in their field. Here's how to approach networking:

- Choose a goal or identify a target industry or employer. People won't be able to help you if you can't specifically tell them what you need.

- Develop a long-term, career-building approach. Who is it important for you to get to know in furthering your career?

- Keep track of the people you meet and make an effort to stay in touch with them through occasional phone calls, notes, e-mails, and even holiday cards.

- Think of others without being asked. That's part of the give-and-take of networking. For example, is there a project someone may want to know about or a relevant newspaper article he or she may not have seen? Or could you help someone else with their career networking by making an introduction or lending your name as a contact?

- Always thank others for their help.

Conducting Informational Interviews

If you suspect that a certain career field might be interesting to you but you don't know enough about it to be sure, conduct an informational interview. Through networking, cold-calling, or personal contacts, find someone who works in your area of interest.

DIVE IN

Call or write this person and make your proposal. Explain that you are not asking for a job but would like to find out about his or her career field. Ask for fifteen to twenty minutes of time and set up an appointment. Be sure to keep your session to that length. Listen carefully during the interview. Jot down a few notes, but save time by writing most of your notes and impressions after the interview is over. Have a copy of your résumé on hand should your interviewer request to see it or to pass it along to a personal contact.

Follow-up is crucial. Immediately after the informational interview, write your contact a brief thank-you letter expressing appreciation for sharing information with you and for putting you in touch with other people in this field. A week later, call the person again to say hello. Thank the person again and ask if he or she has heard of any openings you should pursue. You may want to touch base with this person every month or so to start your network and to keep your contact strong.

In summary, remember the cardinal rules of informational interviewing:

- Be prepared.

- Be brief and courteous.

- Do not ask for a job.

- Follow up with a thank-you letter and an occasional phone call.

Following these tips can help you feel confident that you're focusing your job search on the right career area and are supplied with fresh, appropriate information.

To get the most out of an informational interview, you'll want to be fully prepared. Research the company and/or field through the Internet, your local library, or any other resource you may have available. Prepare a list of questions to bring to your interview. Don't feel the need to be strictly confined to your list. Rather, in the interview, pay close attention to the conversation and focus on the areas that seem most relevant and interesting to you. What follows is a list of general questions you can use to get started.

■ Sample Questions for the Informational Interview

1. Tell me about being a _____ .

2. What do you do in a typical day?

3. Which duties do you like most? Least?

4. How did you get into this field?

5. How is this field changing?

6. How do most people prepare for this job? What skills are needed?

7. What are the entry-level positions?

8. What other jobs are related to this one? Are there any particularly interesting specialties within this field?

9. How do people in this position go about advancing their careers?

10. What education or training is necessary for this position?

11. What personality traits are needed to be successful in this field?

12. What salary range could a person starting in this field expect?

13. Who/which companies are prominent in this field?

14. Could you give me names of people I might contact about an opening in this field?

15. May I use your name in my introduction?

EXERCISE

EXERCISE Write a few other questions you might ask:

16. _____

17. _____

18. _____

19. _____

After doing your research, you should be able to add some more specific questions.

118 Blue Street
Atlanta, GA 01112

September 4, 1997

Ms. Karen O'Donnell
Appraiser
Carver Company, Inc.
Atlanta, GA 01112

Dear Ms. O'Donnell:

I just wanted to take a moment to thank you for your time last week. I appreciated the opportunity to learn about your many responsibilities as a real estate appraiser for Carver Company.

As I pursue my own career in appraising, I will keep in mind the information you were able to provide me. Your advice will certainly come in handy.

Sincerely,

Susan Johns

Susan Johns

Sample Thank-You Letter for an Informational Interview

Should You Relocate for a Job?

Depending on where you live, there may or may not be opportunities in your field. Many of the best professional positions continue to be concentrated in major metropolitan areas such as New York, Chicago, Boston, and Los Angeles. When deciding how to embark on your new career, it is important to consider not just the type of job you want but also the place where you would most like to live and work. You can obtain profiles of different communities at the library in books such as *U.S. Census Data, The Book for the States,* and *Municipal Yearbook.* Check the Internet for information about regions you're considering. If you zero in on a particular area, be sure to call the local chamber of commerce, which can provide you with literature, often at no charge.

EXERCISE

Answer the following questions if you are considering relocating for a position.

1. Where would you *like* to live for the next five to ten years?

2. How appealing are the educational, social, and cultural activities of the area?

3. What are the psychological costs of moving? Do you think you'll be able to adjust? Will you be leaving family and friends behind? What impact will this have on your family?

4. What is the quality and quantity of career opportunities in the new area?

5. Would it be best to relocate now as you embark on your new career or to wait until you've gained some on-the-job experience?

6. Are you able to conduct a job hunt in another community?

7. Is there any chance you could work for a company and then be relocated, at its expense, to another area?

Answer the following questions to determine the financial costs of relocating. If you're unsure of exact numbers, guess on the high side to be safe. Take the total costs into consideration when deciding whether you can afford to make your move.

1. What is the relative cost of living, and will you be able to find a position that covers these costs? (This is extremely important to know because of the wide variation between locations. A "good" salary in Boise, Idaho, will not necessarily afford you a similar lifestyle in New York City or Los Angeles.) Include housing, food, parking, and entertainment expenses in your calculation. Many career web sites now include salary information that can help you compare wages in different regions.

2. Will commuting costs be a factor in the new location?

3. What will it cost you to leave your current housing situation (i.e., breaking a lease or selling a home), and what will it cost you to get into a new home (i.e., security deposit on an apartment or down payment on a new home)?

4. How much are moving expenses? Call a moving company or truck-rental facility to get an estimate. Is it realistic to think that your employer (if you have one) might cover these costs?

5. Will you have any job-search costs as you seek a new position in a new area?

6. Do you have a spouse or significant other who will be relocating with you and will incur expenses finding new work?

7. What are the costs of child care or schools?

Once you have a total of your potential expenses, consider how long your finances will allow you to job hunt. Unless you have a job lined up, it would be unrealistic to think you'll move to a new area and find immediate employment.

Long-Distance Job Hunting

The first decision you'll have to make is whether to job hunt first and then move once you've found a position, or to move and then job hunt. If you can get a job first, that is obviously the best option. Unfortunately, it can be extremely difficult to job hunt long-distance. Most companies today have a sufficient supply of good candidates right in their local area. They can more easily interview local candidates and hire them without the problems and expense of relocating an out-of-the-area employee.

To find job listings out of your area, be sure to check out the Internet. Many career sites offer you the ability to search want ads by location. Also, many newspapers from around the country post their classified ads on the web. Of course, libraries are also an excellent resource for out-of-town newspapers and trade publications with classified ad sections.

If you must have a job before you can relocate, try to spend weekends and vacations in the new city. Do as much research as you can before you make the trip, and line up interviews if possible. Be sure to explain to a potential employer that you plan to move to the city when hired. It may take a long time to obtain a job this way, so be prepared for a lengthy job search.

If you relocate first, begin job hunting as soon as you can. It could take a while to learn the ropes in a new city, and you'll want to land a position before your finances run out. Consider taking a temporary position or contract position to help you buy some time and maybe even meet a potential employer. Then follow the usual steps in job hunting.

If you want to work abroad, beware of scams. Some companies advertise that they have listings of overseas jobs. After you send money for the list, the company often doesn't respond or sends a meaningless, outdated list of multinational companies.

Most U.S. companies looking to fill an international position will hire from within. Since the cost of transferring employees across country borders is expensive—traditionally three to five times salary—corporations seek individuals who first have the necessary technical or managerial expertise, and, second, have a proven record of success within the company. Unless you have a unique skill, significant international experience, and can speak a foreign language fluently, your best bet, if you desire an international position, is to go to work for a multinational company, prove yourself, and keep your eyes open for an in-house opportunity.

Relocation, both within the United States and abroad, can be challenging, but those who do it successfully can greatly increase their employment opportunities and accelerate the progress of their careers.

CHAPTER 5

Have You
Considered . . . ?

Federal Jobs

Should you consider a federal job? Absolutely. Leave out the federal government in your job search and you've eliminated the nation's largest employer. The federal government has seventeen million employees. That's more employees than the first sixteen of the Fortune 500 companies added together and over 2.5 percent of the nation's civilian work force. One in seven Americans works for the federal, state, or local government. And despite attempts at downsizing, the federal government alone hires seven hundred new workers a day.

■ Types of Federal Jobs

Federal employees do every kind of job imaginable. Among their ranks you'll find statisticians, accountants, engineers, pharmacists, lawyers, law enforcement officers, social workers, economists, artists, researchers, bus drivers, teachers, and morticians. In all, there are more than a thousand occupations. Federal employees work in offices, warehouses, shipyards, national parks, hospitals, laboratories, embassies, military bases, and many other places all over the country and around the world.

Don't think that you need to move to Washington, D.C., to get a job with the federal government. Actually, only 10 percent of federal employees work there. Federal employees work in every state, although 35 percent are based in or near the following ten major cities: Atlanta, Boston, Chicago, Dallas, Denver, Kansas City, New York City, Philadelphia, San Francisco, and Seattle.

College degrees are held by 37 percent of the total federal work force. Certain jobs require a four-year bachelor's degree, a graduate degree, or a specific educational concentration.

■ Why Consider a Federal Job?

Job security is a primary reason to consider government work. Federal employment is generally not affected by cyclical fluctuations in the economy. Layoffs, called reduction in force, have occurred in the past; however, they are uncommon and generally affect relatively few workers. Excellent pay and benefits, as good or better than the private sector, are another reason many people seek federal employment.

■ Finding Federal Jobs

The Office of Personnel Management has automated its application process. This means that you, the job seeker, can get application forms and information about federal job vacancies easier and faster than ever before.

Consider working for the United States government. One in seven Americans is employed
by federal, state, and local governments. Their ranks include every type of job imaginable.
(© David Ball/The Stock Market)

Several sources exist for job applicants. Each system supplies information on
worldwide federal job vacancies and application processes and is updated daily.
You can access this information in four ways:

1. **A touch-screen computer found in federal employment information cen-
    ters, state employment offices, and some federal personnel offices.** A very
    user-friendly system, it features easy-to-read menus and maps to search for
    federal vacancies. If you find a job you're interested in, just touch the appro-
    priate box to print the job announcement right off the screen. The printout
    has the name of a person to contact for additional details about the job, basic
    qualifying information, and even the salary range.

2. **Career America Connection.** This is a telephone system, teleservice center, and recruiting message service you can reach by calling (912) 757-3000. Extremely convenient, the system is available twenty-four hours a day, seven days a week. When you call, be sure to have a paper and pencil handy so you can write down the numbers you must punch in to access the various categories of information. For each area you select, you will be led through an additional series of choices. Calls average about six minutes each. Keep in mind that this is a toll call. Federal job information is offered for the hearing impaired using national and regional TDD (Telephone Device for the Deaf) job hotlines.

INTERNET

3. **The Internet.** The U.S. Department of Commerce maintains a site that lists positions across the nation. You can limit your search to specific areas or do a cross-country search for openings at www.fedworld.gov/jobs/jobsearch.html.

Another site provides the political insider's guide to landing federal government jobs. Called *The Plum Book,* otherwise known as the *United States Government Policy and Supporting Positions,* it catalogs more than eight thousand executive and staff positions. The book is released every four years in the weeks following a presidential election. You can go to the library for a copy or look it up on the Internet. The Office of Personnel Management has also put a version of the same information on its web site at www.usa-jobs.opm.gov/.

Do a search for federal jobs using your Internet browser and you may stumble onto additional useful information.

■ Check Out Local Government Positions, Too

Over ten million people, more than half of all government workers, are employed in local government positions. Some of the segments within local government include county government, school districts, fire and police districts, and park districts. The turnover rate for local government positions averages a steep 14 percent. That means lots of job openings at any one time.

Call your local state employment office to learn about available positions. Or visit www.statejobs.com. It is a collection of links to both federal and state job op-

INTERNET portunities.

Working for a Nonprofit Organization

With more than 10 percent of the U.S. work force employed in the nonprofit sector, you may want to give serious consideration to nonprofit organizations in your job search. Why work for a nonprofit company? Nonprofit employees often report a high degree of job satisfaction and personal fulfillment. Nonprofit employees often say they enjoy the diversity of their work. Since budgets are often constrained, one individual may be responsible for many different tasks.

On the downside, most nonprofit employees earn less than their counterparts in for-profit companies, and the pay gap between men and women tends to be more pronounced than in profit companies.

Working for a nonprofit organization can be an end in itself, or it can serve as a steppingstone to other types of work. If you're interested in a job with a nonprofit organization, know that opportunities abound. However, because of their limited recruiting budgets, nonprofits often rely on contacts and referrals when hiring. The implication is clear: If you are looking for a job in the nonprofit sector, you'll have to do more than read the classified ads in the newspaper.

Begin by clarifying your goals. What issues interest you? Here are just a few examples of general issues:

- homelessness
- religion
- hunger
- education
- diseases
- poverty
- the arts

What group of people would you like to work on behalf of? Again, here are a few examples:

- children
- the disabled
- the elderly
- homeless families
- refugees
- the mentally ill
- abuse survivors

Next, learn which organizations focus on these issues. Seek out directories of nonprofit organizations at your library or search the Internet. You might also contact your local United Way chapter. Because the United Way disperses money to numerous nonprofit organizations, it often keeps the most comprehensive list. Your local chamber of commerce may also be familiar with nonprofit organizations in your area.

Use trade publications creatively. Don't review only current postings for a job. Check out old job listings to identify organizations rather than specific positions. Consider using the articles in trade publications to identify organizations that have just received additional funding or are working on a new initiative. Look for stories about changes in leadership. New leaders often make staffing changes and add new positions.

Ultimately, you'll want to research the issues, missions, and methods of specific organizations, continually asking yourself how your interests and skills might fit into an organization's goals.

Then apply all the traditional job-seeking skills you've learned. Set up some informational interviews, begin networking, send out cover letters, and do cold-calling.

On the Internet, visit the following nonprofit sites to research organizations and browse through job databases:

- Action without borders (www.idealist.org)

- Nonprofit Career Network (www.nonprofitcareer.com)

- Opportunity NOCs (www.tmcenter.org)

- Philanthropy Journal Online (jobs.pj.org)

If you have already identified several nonprofit organizations whose missions appeal to you, visit their home pages, where they may list their job openings. Find those web sites using a search engine or by calling the organization itself and asking for its web address.

If you find an organization that you feel would be a perfect fit but no openings exist, consider volunteering your time. Volunteering for a nonprofit organization is an excellent way to prove your commitment, verify your career choice, and make the contacts that will lead to a paying job.

DIVE IN

Working for a Small Company

While it may look better on your résumé and be more impressive to your friends and relatives to say you have a job at a large, well-known company, there are many benefits of working for a small business. First, you'll likely have more responsibilities at a small company. You'll wear many hats, making the job challenging, interesting, and a great learning opportunity. Second, you'll probably have more control over your areas of responsibility. There will be less hierarchy with which to contend and less formal means of authorization. You'll be able to develop an idea and see it through to completion, probably without interference from various departments and superiors. Third, it's easier to get hired at a small company when you have limited experience. Presumably, there are fewer candidates applying for positions than for those at prestigious, big companies. Also, a small company may not be able to afford greatly experienced help. They'll accept entry-level hires knowing that those employees will need to do some of their learning on the job.

When you earch for a small-company employer, don't forget to consider start-up companies. While they may not offer job security (many new businesses eventually fail), they can provide an unsurpassed learning experience, not to mention the pride you'll feel in helping to create something.

Starting Your Own Business

It's the dream of many—to be your own boss and make lots of money. Of course it's easier said than done. But that doesn't mean you should rule out your potential for entrepreneurship. Consider the positives:

1. You're in charge of your own destiny. You make the decisions and don't have to deal with corporate politics and red tape.

2. You control your time—both how many hours and which hours of the day or night. (This can be a terrific perk if you tend to do your best work at odd hours or have young children.)

3. You have the opportunity for great diversity. As an entrepreneur, you may find yourself doing everything from sales, to production, to accounting, tasks that might otherwise be split among specialized employees.

4. To some degree, you have control over your salary.

Now consider the negatives:

1. You get to make the decisions, but you also suffer the consequences of those decisions.

2. Self-employment often means long hours since, ultimately, you are responsible for everything.

3. You will have to be a jack-of-all-trades, overseeing every aspect of the business, at least while in the start-up phase.

4. Because you are on your own, you do not have the support system of co-workers and an established organization.

5. Cash flow can be a serious problem for small businesses. In tough times, your salary is often the first expense to go.

6. Stress over the business's success rides on your shoulders.

7. Because of the risks, job security is low, and the potential for failure is high.

Now take a look at the personality traits you'll need to be an entrepreneur:

1. High energy level

2. Self-motivation

3. Comfort taking risks

4. Able to make a long-range commitment

5. Enjoyment of problem solving

6. High goals

7. Optimism

8. Ability to cope with setbacks

9. Self-confidence

10. Common sense

Do you think you have what it takes to make it as an entrepreneur? You just might if you have a marketable skill or product and the sales ability to get customers. In fact, new businesses are being started at an incredible rate. The increase over just a few years ago is due to a variety of factors, including the trend of downsizing in corporations, which has pushed many midlevel managers and sales and marketing people into the job market; minorities and women who believe they can get ahead faster in their own business than in traditional companies; and modern technology, which makes starting a business cheaper and easier than ever before.

Although the types of businesses change with the economy and technology, the fundamentals of entrepreneurship stay the same. If you'd like to pursue starting your own business, begin by doing market research. Choose a viable business with a product or service in demand. Develop a business plan and thoroughly investigate the feasibility of its implementation. Contact the local office of the Small Business Administration for information and resources for start-ups. Be prepared to work long hours and not take a salary in the beginning (and maybe not for a few years). Start modestly and grow slowly.

INTERNET

You may find the following Internet sites helpful: The Service Corps of Retired Executives at www.score.org offers small-business advice and access via e-mail to over one hundred counselors who can provide personalized assistance; the Small Business Administration at www.sbaonline.sba.gov outlines the federal agency's resources and offers an on-line checklist for starting a business; Svoboda's Home & Small Business Interactive at www.svobodamag.com provides practical small-business advice through several free columns; Smart Business Supersite at www.smartbiz.com is a how-to resource site for small businesses; and Start Up University.com (www.startupuniversity.com) is a clearinghouse of links to many other useful entrepreneurial sites.

In the United States, only 30 percent of all start-ups are still in business after five years. The more you prepare yourself and understand the challenges ahead, the better your chances for success.

EXERCISE

Answer the following questions:

1. Do you think you may have what it takes to start your own business?

2. If so, which of the qualities of an entrepreneur do you possess? Which do you lack?

3. What other qualities have you observed in successful businesspeople you know or know about?

4. Do you think starting your own business might be a realistic option for you? Why or why not?

5. If you were to choose to become an entrepreneur, what type of business do you think you might want?

Taking a Different Job Path

Having trouble finding a job that's in line with your chosen career? How about changing direction? Perhaps you have a secondary career interest or a hobby that you could pursue in the job market, at least on a short-term basis.

While taking a direct route up the corporate ladder to your dream job is everyone's first choice, sometimes that isn't possible. A job isn't necessarily a career. And a job that isn't quite the right fit doesn't have to be a waste of time. You can still learn from your surroundings, make contacts, and gain valuable work experience from every position you hold. Furthermore, employers are more likely to hire someone who already has a job.

Don't become stressed if it takes you a while to figure out exactly what you most want to do or to obtain that perfect job. You may have several jobs before you find your passion. And you'll quickly discover what you don't want to do. Talk with anyone who has been in the working world for more than a few years and ask them about their first jobs. While they may recount some horror stories, most will also tell you the value of those early experiences.

Sometimes you can find a job that has a loose connection to your chosen career, like the grade school teacher who works for the first few years in a day care center, the landscape architect who works for a florist, the physical therapist who works as a personal trainer in a gym, or the chef who works in a grocery store. Other times, that first job will be a major departure from your career choice, like the actor who waits tables in a restaurant, a dental hygienist who works in a real estate office, or a paralegal who works for a stock brokerage firm.

Remember that first jobs are not likely to be where you will spend the rest of your career. During the time that you're working in your less-than-perfect job, you can always continue the search for a position in your field, all while earning an income and learning something new.

EXERCISE **EXERCISE**

1. Briefly describe your dream job. _____

2. List at least two different directions outside your primary career choice that you could consider for employment, at least on a short-term basis. To develop this answer, think of your minor in college, favorite elective classes, hobbies, clubs you belong to, and any special talents you have.

_____

_____

3. Read through the Sunday classified section of your daily newspaper and circle at least two positions outside of your chosen career that sound interesting to you.

Now you can decide whether the time is right for you to apply for those jobs you selected out of the newspaper or whether to employ some of the other job-hunting techniques described in this book to help you find a position outside your primary career choice.

Further Education

One of the most valuable assets to today's employers is an employee who has demonstrated the ability to learn and to continue learning. Perhaps your immediate future might have you sitting in a classroom instead of a boardroom.

Although many recent graduates shudder at the thought of spending even another minute doing homework, further education or training might be an essential element of your successful job search. Just be certain you're not choosing to continue your education simply to avoid the potential rejection that comes with job hunting. Some questions to ask yourself:

1. Are you undereducated in comparison to others in your field? In some specialties, a master's or doctoral degree is common and necessary in order to stay truly competitive. Interview employers in your field, read the classifieds, and network to find out what it takes to keep up with your peers.

2. Are your skills rusty? Are you stranded in the breakdown lane of the information superhighway? Is the most complicated thing you've written able to fit on a Post-it note? Perhaps now is the time to invest in yourself and your career potential. Many local colleges have refresher courses ranging in length from an afternoon to weeks or years. Start with a simple goal, such as auditing a computer course at a local community college or adult education center, and see how quickly you can regain your skills as well as your self-confidence.

3. Do you have a burning desire to know more about widgets? Or topiary? Or Shakespeare? Some of the most exciting and profitable learning that can occur begins with a unique, personal interest. Many people are curious about certain subjects. Quenching those curiosities through a seminar, course, certificate program, or degree may be the beginning of a wonderful new career direction.

4. Will another degree or certificate make you more valuable to current or potential employers? Could you go even further in your current position if you took the plunge and signed up for a few classes? Would additional education or training enable you to apply for new positions within the company? Some-

times the only thing that is preventing an escape from a dead-end job is a few new skills. Inquire at your work place to see what training or education is needed to secure positions that are appealing to you.

5. Do you need to pass an exam, get a license, or get certified? Many professions separate the professionals from the amateurs with professional licensing exams or certifications. Yet many in those fields remain in lower-paying jobs despite having all or most of the skills to move ahead because they are intimidated by the rigors of passing a test or taking a course. It might be time to muster your courage and study up for the big test. Take a refresher course or study with a colleague if these things help you to take the next step. Ask yourself what you have to lose. If the answer is nothing, then get started today.

DIVE IN

Taking Your Job Hunt On-Line

Pounding the Virtual Pavement

■ The New Medium for Job Seekers

Although reading classified ads, cold-calling, letter writing, and networking have traditionally been the most widely used means of finding a job, the Internet has fast emerged as an important tool in the job-search process. With its expansive resources of easily accessible information, its powerful searching capabilities, and its instant channels of communication, it has begun to revolutionize the way people look for jobs and the way companies recruit.

■ What Is the Internet?

The Internet is a vast system of millions of interconnected computer networks. This global network links individuals, businesses, universities, libraries, and governments throughout the world. And, unlike virtually any other medium, no one owns or operates it—it's just there. Although the Internet was a government initiative started in the 1960s, its boom in the commercial and educational markets in the past few years has sparked new ways for doing business and communicating across the world.

The World Wide Web is the fastest-growing part of the Internet. By using a viewer, called a web browser, people can retrieve information from web sites that other companies or individuals have created. HTML (hypertext markup language) is the formatting language used to create web pages and establish hypertext links to other web sites. Most web browsers allow users to view text, graphics, video, and animation on the web as well as hear audio. It is also possible to download software programs, conduct on-line discussions, and purchase items on the web.

■ Using the Internet to Job Hunt

For your purposes as a job seeker, the Internet can provide great tools to assist in your search. You can network; exchange correspondence; gather research on careers, trends, industries, and individual companies; search for job openings; post your résumé; get career advice from professional counselors; and exchange ideas with other job hunters. What's more, the Internet is being used by many prominent companies to list job openings, accept employee applications, and even conduct interviews on-line. In fact, it has been called the future of recruiting.

■ It's Fast; It's Convenient

One of the best aspects about the Internet is its convenience. You can go on-line at any time; it's "open" twenty-four hours a day. If doing your research or networking best fits your schedule in the evening or on weekends, no problem. Unlike a library or business, the Internet is there whenever you need it.

You should keep in mind, though, that not all information you find on the Internet is accurate, current, or necessarily true. Be sure to carefully evaluate the quality of Internet data you gather before using it to make an important decision.

■ Show Employers You Know Your Way Around the Internet

Although your level of success on the Internet depends in part on the kind of job you're looking for and how skilled you are in on-line computing, the Internet should still be a major component of your job search. Beyond listing specific job openings, it is an invaluable research tool.

At the very least, job seekers who conduct a cybersearch demonstrate to employers a basic knowledge of personal computers. In today's intensely competitive job market, every little advantage counts.

■ Accessing the Internet

If you don't have a computer, don't despair. Many public libraries and most schools offer Internet access through their computers. Take advantage of free resources before making a big investment in your own computer equipment.

If you do have your own computer and are a student, you can most likely get on-line free of charge through your school. Inquire at your school's computer center to obtain any necessary software and learn what requirements you must meet.

If you are not a student, to get on-line you'll need a personal computer, a modem (most newer computers have built-in modems), an Internet service provider, and a browser to view the World Wide Web. You can use one of the service providers that offers the Internet and e-mail (electronic mail) only, or use one of the on-line services that provide Internet access as well as many other on-line capabilities, like America Online. Service charges vary according to many factors, but typically range from $10 to $25 a month for unlimited use.

Use the Internet to boost your job search in the following ways:

■ Get Wired, Get Hired

Industry research. Begin by checking trade periodicals. Most publications have their own web sites that highlight key stories relevant to the industry. Next, find the industry's main web sites by checking major indexes like Yahoo! at www.yahoo.com, and Excite at www.excite.com. Finally, search for discussion groups in the chosen industry. These groups often produce discussion lists about industry-related information and often keep back issues at their web sites. A good search engine for finding these types of mailing lists is Liszt Select at www.liszt.com.

Company research.   If you have identified a specific company as your potential employer, you'll want to know everything you can about it to help better target your cover letter and to appear knowledgeable in an interview. Begin by finding the company's own web site, as most companies now have them. Try doing a search using the company's name and then end it with .com. If that doesn't bring up the site you seek, try a keyword search using a major search engine like AltaVista (www.altavista.digit.com), which has a special "Find a Business" area. You can also often find the company's web site address listed in any of its ads and promotional literature. If you still strike out, just give the company itself a call. Most companies will gladly give out their web address over the phone with no questions asked.

Some career services have a section called Employer Profiles, where you find detailed information on employers around the world. Or try Hoover's Online at www.hoovers.com/, which is the best source for on-line company profiles.

If the company in which you're interested is publicly held, check out its stock. Information like its general price range and recent history can help you assess how the company is doing. Go to Yahoo! (www.yahoo.com) and click on the stock quotes link. Then type in the name of the company. For more detailed financial information, you can locate the SEC (Securities and Exchange Commission) filings of public companies at the EDGAR database.

Finally, one other key way of learning about an individual company is becoming familiar with its competitors. Once again, Hoover's Online (www.hoovers.com) is a first-rate resource. If a company is listed in Hoover, often its competitors, and hyperlinks to their web sites, will be referenced.

Job openings databases.   Every day, the various career sites download and index job postings. The organization of these databases continually improves so that you can use these powerful tools to search postings by location, job title, and skills required. See the list of career sites at the end of this chapter.

Résumé banks.   You can enter your résumé into a data bank where it is available to human resources professionals and recruiters. Be sure to investigate what type of employer might search this particular résumé bank before posting your résumé with it. Also, find out how long your résumé stays on-line. Most résumé banks provide this information on their web site or will answer specific questions by e-mail.

On-line career discussion groups.   Discussion groups, also known as Usenet, are on-line groups in which you exchange information with other job seekers and professionals through text messages. You enter a "chat room," where you can ask questions, give and get advice, share war stories, exchange leads, and obtain information from specialists in different fields. To find a discussion group that's right for you, go to the Deja News search engine (www.dejanews.com) and click on "Search for Interests" link to obtain a list of relevant groups. Liszt Select at www.liszt.com also provides links to career discussion groups.

Most schools and public libraries provide Internet access through their computers.
(© Spencer Grant/Photo Researchers, Inc.)

Electronic bulletin boards. Like a corkboard in your local grocery store or
laundromat, these boards are for posting and reading notices. They provide thousands of help wanted classifieds and also enable job seekers to post their
résumés. Most electronic bulletin boards charge nothing for their services; the
few that charge nominal fees usually provide more services, such as categorizing
your résumé for easy access to employers or ensuring confidentiality. Job listings
are run by individuals, associations, civic groups, and corporations. There are a
lot of them, so be prepared to sift through to find the ones relevant to your situation. To find these bulletin boards, start by visiting some of the major career sites
listed at the end of this chapter.

Newspaper classifieds. No longer are you restricted to looking at the classified ads in your local newspaper. Many major newspapers, including the *New
York Times, The Washington Post, The Chicago Tribune, The Los Angeles Times, The Boston Globe,* and many smaller newspapers now post their classified employment
ads on-line. You can go to the web site for the individual publication or visit a
general site like CareerPath.com, which condenses the classifieds of several hun-

dred newspapers into a single location that can be searched by category of work or location.

Career guidance and job-search help.   Nearly all commercial on-line services and the Internet have areas devoted exclusively to helping job seekers manage their searches. These sites often include résumé templates, articles about job searching and career management, and discussion forums about careers. See the list of career sites at the end of this chapter.

Your own web page.   On your résumé and in your cover letters, you can refer to your personal home page. This is a great place to strut your stuff. The average size is usually about four to twenty pages. Use your web page to give more detailed information about your background and include work samples, photos, letters of recommendation, and anything else that will demonstrate to a prospective employer that you're the right person for the job. Many books and software packages are available to help you create your own web site, or you can enlist the assistance of a professional web designer.

E-mail.   Electronic-mail messages are a key component of modern communications, ranking right up there with the telephone, traditional paper mail, and facsimile (fax) machines. One of the nice things about e-mail is that you can directly address your communication to an individual and have a better chance of having it reach him or her directly without interference from a secretary or other type of gatekeeper. Your e-mail will go directly to that individual's computer. Furthermore, you're more likely to receive a response. The professional is already seated at the computer and can simply dash off a quick, informal e-mail reply to your request.

E-mail is an excellent tool to find out if a position has been filled, show initial interest in a job, request more information, and inquire about the status of a position you've applied for. It's fast, easy, and amazingly effective. To increase the chances that your e-mail will generate action, be sure it contains the following items: a statement that clearly identifies the purpose of the e-mail; relevant facts to support the purpose; a request specifying the next step to be taken; and a time frame in which you would appreciate a reply.

Career products and services.   You can search through hundreds of ads to locate products or services that might prove useful in your job search. Books, résumé software, and networking services are just a few examples.

Salary research.   Salary guides on the Internet can help you develop a realistic picture of what you might expect to earn. That information can be invaluable to you in negotiating for your position. Many major career sites contain salary data.

Learning about an area.   You can use the Internet to obtain data on a specific place you may be considering for employment. For example, you can learn about the cost of living, housing options, and schools in that area.

Some advice for the hesitant.   Don't be intimidated by computers and the Internet. Both are more user friendly than ever before. There are plenty of books on the market to help you get started if you need a little push. Also, the Internet has gained global acceptance, so one of your friends or teachers can no doubt offer advice or help. Don't put off using this valuable tool.

■ Searching the Internet

Finding the information you need on the Internet can be a little like searching for a needle in a haystack. Search engines are programs that help you do your research. They act almost like a card catalog in a library.

Literally hundreds of search engines exist. Some search the web at large while others have a narrower focus and search a specific database. And not all search engines are created equal. They're specialists that have different strengths and weaknesses. That's why you'll want to try your searches in more than one search engine.

Search engines have a search box, which is the space you use to type in keywords or search phrases. To make your search more precise, use three or four keywords connected by *and* rather than a single word. A single-word search can result in thousands of matches, which will be more than you want to see. Almost every search engine has a help section that describes exactly how to get the best results. It's worth taking the time to read those directions. Some of the most thorough search engines are:

- AltaVista (www.altavista.digital.com)
- Excite (www.excite.com)
- Galaxy (www.einet.net/galaxy.html)
- HotBot (www.hotbot.com)
- Infoseek (www.infoseek.com)
- Lycos (www.lycos.com)
- Search.com (www.search.com)
- Yahoo! (www.yahoo.com)

The Internet Sleuth at www.isleuth.com can search multiple databases at the same time, including AltaVista, Excite, Infoseek, and Yahoo.

■ The Right Site

Information on the Internet changes daily, even hourly, so sites listed here can quickly become out-of-date. To get the most current information, you can do your own research on-line. Surfing the Internet is fun and educational.

You might also try your local bookstore or library. There are many books that, like traditional phone books, provide current Internet addresses.

In the interest of getting you started, here are addresses for some of the top sites related to job hunting and careers valid at the time of this book's publication:

- America's CareerInfoNet—www.acinet.org
- America's Employers—www.americasemployers.com
- America's Job Bank—www.ajb.dni.us
- America's Talent Bank—www.atb.org
- Career City—www.careercity.com
- Career Magazine—www.careermag.com
- Career Mosaic—www.careermosaic.com
- Careers Online—www.careersonline.com
- Career Shop—www.careershop.com
- Career Site—www.careersite.com
- CareerPath.com—www.careerpath.com
- Headhunter—www.headhunter.net
- HotJobs.com—www.hotjobs.com
- Job Net—www.jobnet.com
- Jobcenter.com—www.jobcenter.com
- JobHunt—www.job-hunt.org
- Monster.com—www.monster.com
- Online Career Center—www.occ.com
- Student Center—www.studentcenter.com
- Yahoo! Classifieds—classifieds.yahoo.com/employment.html

CHAPTER 7

Writing
Cover Letters

Elements of the Cover Letter

When most people think of job hunting, they tend to focus on preparing their résumé. In fact, the cover letter deserves as much, if not more, attention in an effective job search. The cover letter is a chance, in narrative form, to introduce yourself, describe your strengths and skills, and express interest in a particular job. More and more, employers are looking at the cover letter as an indicator of your writing skill. A well-written cover letter can help you stand out from the masses. It encourages the potential employer to give consideration to your résumé and, ultimately, to interview you for the position.

From a technical standpoint, your cover letter is a way to indicate your formal application for a specific position. Therefore, it is also called a letter of application and is usually accompanied by your résumé. A cover letter comprises three main elements:

1. **Introductory paragraph.** The first paragraph mentions the position you're interested in and how you've learned of the opening (if indeed you have learned of an opening). If a friend or business contact told you about the position, mention his or her name, and be sure to send him or her a copy of your letter. In this paragraph, you may also want to specify why you're applying to this particular company (i.e., because of its outstanding reputation in the field). This paragraph may be two to four sentences long.

   If you are sending a mass mailing to many companies over a large area, along with focusing on the type of position you seek, introduce some of the abilities you have that will be of interest to an employer. If you are sending a cover letter to a specific company and don't know whether there is an opening, begin by explaining what type of position you want and why you are especially interested in working for that company.

2. **Body.** In the middle two paragraphs you should plan to "toot your own horn," honestly of course. In this section, be sure to mention at least three of your strong points. A good technique is to use one paragraph to explain your educational background and another paragraph to describe your work experience. The more specifics you can list, the better. Also make mention of other qualities that suggest you're a highly desirable employee. Are you energetic, enthusiastic, detail oriented, a fast learner? Choose adjectives that are applicable to the position you want. Use the body of your cover letter to make a connection to the employer.

3. **Closing.** Don't forget the overall purpose of sending your cover letter and résumé: to obtain an interview. Be sure to indicate specifically and assertively what you want the employer to do next. "I'd like to arrange an interview at your earliest convenience" is a clear statement. Make mention of how and where you can be reached, or indicate that you'll call the employer on a specific day. The tone should be polite yet explicit regarding what you expect the next step in the process to be.

The Write Stuff

Keep these tips in mind when writing your cover letters:

KEY POINT

1. **The best cover letters reveal your enthusiasm for a particular job and tell the employer why you are worthy of consideration.** The cover letter is your initial "knock on the door," your chance to make that all-important first impression. In today's highly competitive job market, your cover letter has to be as dynamic and impressive as your résumé . . . and your personality.

2. **Don't send a résumé without a cover letter.** Why pass up an opportunity to present your best qualities? That's what a cover letter is. It puts your résumé in context, drawing attention to your strengths and best attributes. It gives you a chance to show your personality in a way that the strictly formatted résumé doesn't allow you. At its most basic level, it allows you to demonstrate your writing skills. Most important, it serves as an introduction to your résumé, a teaser that encourages the reader to take the time to learn more about you.

3. **Personalize your cover letter.** If you address your letter to a specific individual rather than "Dear Sir," "To Whom It May Concern," or "Human Resources Department," your letter has a much better chance of being read. To get the name of an individual, call the company for information, check the library for trade publications and reference materials that list company officers, search the Internet for company information, or do your best to find out from a personal contact who may have the inside scoop. Invest your energy in doing solid research to better aim your cover letter at a target person who can make a hiring decision.

4. **Make sure your letter looks professional.** Type your letter, and be sure to spell-check it. Typos, misspellings, grammatical errors, and cross-outs immediately say to the reader that you lack written communication skills and don't pay attention to detail. If you are unsure of your writing abilities, ask a professor, coworker, or friend to proofread your work. Even the best writers have editors; enlist several of your own.

5. **Keep your letter to one page.** Your cover letter should be concise but thorough. The length will depend on the amount of content you have to convey, but a total of three to six paragraphs should allow you to cover the most important points. Devote one paragraph to each key thought. Short paragraphs (no more than four or five sentences) make your letter easy to read.

6. **Familiarize yourself with standard letter formats.** The sample letters in this chapter follow standard rules for spacing and punctuation. Demonstrate your written communication skills by creating a professional-looking and professional-sounding letter. If you are unsure of proper letter format, copy one of the samples in this chapter. Many find the full-block format, as used in the sample letter written to Jennifer Yardley on p. 103 the easiest to follow.

A résumé should always be accompanied by a cover letter that expresses your enthusiasm for a specific job and clearly states why you are a worthy candidate. (© David Young-Wolff/PhotoEdit)

7. **Make your cover letter scannable.** Today's cover letters are often read not only by humans but also by computers. They are scanned into applicant databases along with résumés. To ensure proper scanning of your letter, use black type on white or off-white paper. Choose an easy-to-read typeface such as Helvetica or Arial in a point size between 8 and 12. Avoid graphics, bold and italic type, and underlining. Mail your letter and résumé paper-clipped, not stapled, unfolded in a 9″ × 12″ envelope.

INTERNET

For more examples of cover letters, investigate Student Center at www.studentcenter.com.

What Not to Write in Your Cover Letter

Here's a humorous collection of sentences that were found on real cover letters. (They were submitted by various human resource departments.)

- I demand a salary commiserate with my extensive experience.
- Wholly responsible for two (2) failed financial institutions.
- Reason for leaving last job: maturity leave.
- It's best for employers that I not work with people
- Let's meet, so you can "ooh" and "aah" over my experience.
- You will want me to be Head Honcho in no time.
- Am a perfectionist and rarely if if ever forget details.
- I was working for my mom until she decided to move.
- I have an excellent track record, although I am not a horse.
- I am loyal to my employer at all costs. . . . Please feel free to respond to my résumé on my office voice mail.
- I have become completely paranoid, trusting completely no one and absolutely nothing.
- My goal is to be a meteorologist. But since I possess no training in meteorology, I suppose I should try stock brokerage.
- I procrastinate, especially when the task is unpleasant.
- Instrumental in ruining entire operation for a Midwest chain store.
- Reason for leaving last job: They insisted that all employees get to work by 8:45 A.M. every morning. I couldn't work under those conditions.
- The company made me a scapegoat, just like my three previous employers.

EXERCISE

A good cover letter takes into account the questions below. Think of the type of position and employer you plan to apply to, and answer the questions accordingly.

1. Who is the person who will most likely read this letter? What type of person is he or she? List at least five descriptive phrases. Of course, if you've never met this person, you will be forced to make some assumptions. The point is that if you're writing a letter to a banker, you should probably phrase your letter more formally than if you were writing a letter to a creative director at an advertising agency.

2. What do you think is important for the reader to know about you?

3. Why will your letter be interesting and important to the reader? What's in it for him or her?

4. What special talents and skills make you a better choice than other applicants?

5. What work experience and educational background do you have that the reader will find significant and relevant?

6. Why would you like to work for the reader's company?

■ Try It!

DIVE IN

Call several local companies in your field. Try to find out the correct name, address, and title of the person you would report to if hired in your ideal position. Develop a list of these contacts. Note any difficulties you have in eliciting this information and determine which strategies work best.

Alternative Letter-Writing Strategies

Because no two prospective employers are alike, there's no one way to write cover letters. When seeking an especially competitive position or when stressing unusual skills or abilities, you might consider an alternative approach to the standard cover-letter format. Your best bet is to take the information you have about the job opening (from a classified ad, personal contact, library or Internet research, etc.) and use it to craft a letter that you think fits the needs of the prospective employer. As with all cover letters, the more you can customize your cover letter, the better. Here are some suggested styles:

- **Problem/Solution.** Identify the employer's need and describe in your letter how you can be the perfect answer to that need.

- **Inverted pyramid.** Read the newspaper and you'll see that most news stories are written this way. Put your most important, most relevant information first. Begin with a statement of your career goal and reasons for interest in the position, and then move into the specifics of why and how you're the best candidate.

- **Deductive order.** Begin your letter with a generalization, almost a thesis statement. Then support that thesis with examples in the body of the letter. For example, describe a specific ability you have. Then give examples of how you demonstrated that skill in a previous job or at school.

- **Inductive order.** This is the reverse of the deductive order. You begin your letter by describing a specific situation in which you've been involved.

Then use that example to draw the general conclusion that you have a particular skill, one that is necessary for success at the job you're applying for.

- **List.** Extremely popular, this is one of the most effective formats because of its readability. Insert a bulleted list in the body of your letter. It may be a list of relevant experience, related skills, or reasons why you think you're a good candidate for the job.

Types of Cover Letters

Because cover letters can be such a wonderful means of communicating with a potential employer, you should seek out opportunities to send them. Because it can be composed at your leisure and with great thought, a letter often gets better results than a phone call. The three most common types of letters you'll send are: (1) the letter to generate a lead (also called a broadcast letter because it may be sent to many potential employers at the same time); (2) the referral letter (also called a networking letter because it uses one contact to make another); and (3) the response to a classified ad.

- **Lead-generating letter.** Use this type of letter when you've identified a company you'd like to work for but don't know if any positions are available. You may send out five to ten of these letters or several hundred, depending on the type of job you want and the breadth of your search. The good news is that if you obtain an interview from a lead-generating letter, you'll probably be one of few (or even the only one) being considered for a position. The bad news is that of the many letters you send, only a small percentage, and maybe none at all, will net a response.

- **Referral letter.** Referral letters often bring excellent results. The mere mention of a mutual contact can get your letter past the secretary's desk to the decision maker. If you are networking effectively, you'll have many opportunities to send out this type of letter.

- **Response to a classified ad.** The best thing about responding to a classified ad is that you know that a position exists. Unfortunately, a classified ad in a major publication can generate hundreds of responses, so your cover letter had better be good.

Sample Letters

You'll find that once you've written one or two cover letters, writing more will be a cinch. In fact, you'll probably be able to use much of the same wording with minor modifications in all your future letters.

EXERCISE

Read the sample cover letters on the following pages. They are written in several different formats, all equally acceptable. Now it's time to create your own. Compose three cover letters. The first one should be a lead-generating letter. The second should be a referral letter. And the third should be a response to a classified ad that you have clipped from a newspaper or trade publication. This assignment may take some time, but rest assured that it is a worthwhile endeavor. Although this is a practice exercise, you may still want to use the name, address, and title of a person you wish to contact later in your job search. Show your letter to instructors, your employers, and friends. Use their feedback to hone your work.

Once you have perfected these three letters, you can use them, or modifications of them, in your actual job search. When you're done with this exercise, it's time to give yourself a hearty pat on the back. You've just completed one of the most arduous tasks of job hunting, the writing of your first cover letters.

14 Hill Street
Middletown, IL 61604
February 24, 2001

Ms. Jennifer Yardley
Vice President
Technopro, Inc.
672 Charles Avenue
Bedford, IL 61604

Dear Ms. Yardley:

Is your company looking for an experienced, detail-oriented bookkeeper? If so, I would very much like to be considered for the position.

In June, I will receive an associate's degree in business from Middletown College. I have been attending school in the evenings while working days as an assistant bookkeeper at Molly's Chinese Restaurant. That experience has enabled me to gain valuable knowledge in bookkeeping while learning the basics of operating a small business.

I would be interested in arranging an interview at your convenience. If you find you do not have an opening at this time, please feel free to pass my résumé along to your colleagues. Thank you for your consideration. I can be reached at 555-8888.

Sincerely,

Christopher George

Christopher George

Enc.

Lead-Generating Letter

Seana Stebbins
3499 West Oak Lane
Clarence, IL 60689
(601) 555-7147
E-mail: sstebbins@prodigy.com

April 4, 2000

Mr. Wallace Reed
Sales Manager
Horace Chemicals, Inc.
111 Orange St.
Clarence, IL 60689

Dear Mr. Reed:

I was the kid on the block with the lemonade stand, the student who won the Brownie camera because I sold the most candy bars, the Girl Scout who went to Disney World for free because I moved the most cookies. Sales has always been my forte.

Now, however, my sales expertise has progressed from cookies and candy to medical technology, specifically pharmaceutical products. I'm writing to see if you might have a need for my skills. Briefly, here's what I would bring to the job:

- 5 years with CapCom Pharmaceuticals as sales representative
- CapCom Salesperson-of-the-Year, 1999, 2000
- Instrumental in the launch of three new pharmaceutical products
- Specialized knowledge in cancer treatments
- M.S. degree in chemistry from Purdue College; B.S. in biology from Notre Dame College

My clients and coworkers would describe me as highly energetic, pleasant to work with, and extremely detail oriented. I would welcome the opportunity to meet with you and discuss how I might fit in as a part of the Horace Chemicals sales team.

Enclosed is my résumé. I will contact you next week to set up an appointment. By the way, I'll bring the lemonade and cookies. Old habits are tough to break.

Sincerely,

Seana Stebbins

Seana Stebbins

Enc: Résumé

Lead-Generating Letter

220 Boulder Drive
Manchester, WY 73104
May 10, 2001

Mr. Glenn Severance
Director of Human Resources
Acme Corporation
802 Maple Street
Allston, WY 70011

Dear Mr. Severance:

Janine Hudson of your Marketing Department recently informed me of the opening for an administrative assistant. I believe that my educational background and my experience in business qualify me for the position. Please consider this letter as my formal application.

On May 24, I will graduate from New England University with an associate's degree in Business Administration. I have up-to-date knowledge in the field, having completed courses in everything from marketing to managerial finance. I have maintained a 3.6 cumulative average while financing my education myself by working part- and full-time jobs.

As you will note on the enclosed résumé, I have several years' background in business. As a secretary at Wallace's, Inc., I've experienced the day-to-day operation of a large manufacturing company such as yours. I've also demonstrated my managerial skills by supervising and training other employees at ComputerMart.

I look forward to discussing my capabilities and potential with you. You can reach me by writing to the above address or calling me at (307) 555-4242.

Sincerely,

Langdon Kenney

Langdon Kenney

Enc.
c: J. Hudson

Referral Letter, Following Up on a Lead

FRANK NAGLE

6688 Glen Haven Circle, Orley Park, VA 44989, (505) 555-3338
Nagle 99@mediaone.com

January 6, 2000

Mr. John Zofchack, Vice President
Manley Accounting Services
2220 Conway Ave.
Charleston, VA 44999

RE: Your controller position (Referred by Marisol Playa)

Dear Mr. Zofchack:

As an accountant with more than five years in the field, I was excited to learn of your need for an experienced controller. Marisol Playa, a former colleague, suggested I contact you. She thought my experience closely matched your job requirements.

Your needs:	My qualifications:
• Four-year degree	• BS in accounting
• CPA credential	• CPA plus additional course work in financial management
• Experience in report generation	• Compiled data for quarterly and annual reports. Generated inventory reports on a weekly basis.
• Accounting software proficiency	• Experience with Excel, Peachtree, Lotus, and various financial analysis programs
• Five years' experience with major accounting firm	• Two years with Whitney Marcel Ltd. as an accountant; three years with Kosmos Corp. as senior accountant/controller

This abbreviated list represents only some of my relevant experience, so I am enclosing my résumé. I am currently employed with Kosmos Corp. but am seeking new and exciting challenges. I will contact you next week in hopes that we can further discuss the requirements of the position. Thank you for your interest.

Sincerely yours,

Frank Nagle

Frank Nagle

Enclosure: Résumé

Referral Letter, Following Up on a Lead

Kimba Bartlett
127 D.W. Highway
Kensington, IL 34333
(405) 555-6784
e-mail: kbartlett@aol.com

June 1, 2000

Mr. Kyle Cooke
Office Manager
Midtown Software, Inc.
575 Island Rd.
Kensington, IL 34333

Dear Mr. Cooke:

I am writing to apply for the position of Administrative Assistant as advertised in the *Kensington Ledger* on May 25, 2000.

For the past year I have worked as a secretary at Royer's Hospital in downtown Kensington. My responsibilities are diverse, including receptionist duties, bookkeeping, word processing, and file management.

At the end of this month I will graduate from Kensington Community College with an associate's degree in liberal arts. I would like to use the skills I've acquired at Royer's combined with my degree from Kensington in an interesting, challenging position.

Enclosed is my résumé. It details the skills I could bring to Midtown Software in the position of administrative assistant. I will contact you next week to discuss how we can explore this possibility further. Thank you for your consideration.

Sincerely,

Kimba Bartlett

Kimba Bartlett

Enclosure: Résumé

Response to Classified Ad

1654 Daige Street
Burbank, CA 99877
March 24, 2001

Box J-97
Burbank Times
Opportunity Plaza
Burbank, CA 99877

Re: Collections Agent Position

Please consider me for the position of collections agent as advertised in the March 20 edition of the *Burbank Times.*

In the past three years, I have had much experience in collections. Frequently, in my position as a customer service representative at Village Bank, I assisted collections clerks with their telephone and written inquiries as well as answered many customer questions regarding past-due accounts. My employers have often complimented me on my attention to detail and my perseverance in solving difficult problems.

I would appreciate the opportunity to further discuss this position and my qualifications. Please contact me for an interview at the above address or at (203) 555-2222.

Sincerely,

Shannon Bourke

Shannon Bourke

Enc.

Response to Classified Ad

CHAPTER
8
Obtaining Letters of Recommendation

References Available upon Request

You have a winning résumé, a dynamic cover letter. Now the finishing touch is some stellar references. References should be more than a list of names for the employer to call. Some employers will make the effort to follow up, but others won't. Positive letters of recommendation can be the ultimate sales tool in getting an employer to choose you.

■ Who Can Give You a Letter of Recommendation?

KEY POINT

The strongest references come from previous employers who can vouch for your knowledge, integrity, and enthusiasm toward work. Your best bet is to get a reference from an immediate supervisor, manager, or coworker. The higher the title, the better. But remember, your reference writer must know who you are and what you did. If you think it would be helpful, you may even want to get references from several people at the company.

Keep in mind that you don't have to have been a full-time employee to get a letter of recommendation. Consider requesting references at places where you were employed part-time, interned, volunteered, or freelanced. Ideally, you should begin gathering letters of recommendation either just before you leave a position or soon afterward, while the quality of your work is still fresh in the mind of the potential letter writer. Request letters only from people who think positively of you. If you believe that your manager is unlikely to give you a good letter, consider asking your immediate supervisor or even a coworker.

Other potential letter writers may include your teachers, guidance counselors, leaders of organizations or clubs, or other people familiar with your work. However, they should all be professional contacts. Personal references from friends, neighbors, or relatives should be rarely used and only in cases in which the employer might need a character reference, such as for positions in child care and law enforcement.

■ How Do You Get a Letter of Recommendation?

The easiest way to get a letter of recommendation is to ask your supervisor or manager. Tell that person about the type of position you plan to apply for so the letter can be better focused toward your objective. Also, as politely as possible, give the writer a deadline to ensure that your letter is treated as a priority.

Remember, although some people are quite adept at letter writing and will be more than willing to write a reference, others may find the task challenging or be so busy they can't do it within your time frame. A tack you can take to help speed the process along and ensure the content of the letter is to follow these steps:

1. Prepare a draft of your letter of recommendation. For your reference writer's convenience, find out what word-processing program he or she uses. Draft the letter on that program and save it on a floppy disk.

2. Hand deliver or mail your reference person both a disk and a printed copy of your recommendation letter. Another option is to e-mail the draft of your recommendation letter. No matter how you choose to submit your materials, be sure to include a cover letter that invites your reference to review your draft, edit it as desired, and return the final draft on company letterhead.

3. After receiving your letter of recommendation, make copies of it. Don't send an original to a prospective employer; you may not get it back.

4. Send a thank-you note to the person who wrote your letter. That note will help ensure a positive referral should the individual be personally contacted by a potential employer seeking additional information.

▪ What Should a Letter of Recommendation Say?

If you are drafting your own letter, be sure to include the following:

1. An identification of your reference—his or her position, how he or she knows you.

2. State who is being recommended (namely you) and for what type of position.

3. Describe the reference's relationship with you—how long you worked together, in what capacity, and specific projects that you shared.

4. List your top skills, qualities, work habits, attributes, and achievements.

5. Mention that the reference can be contacted for additional information.

6. If your reference person prefers to write his or her own letter, verbally review the above points to ensure the effectiveness of the letter. A letter of recommendation lacking that information won't help your case.

▪ How Many Recommendations Are Enough?

Six references should be the maximum, but even one or two can help to sway a prospective employer. Rather than quantity, focus on quality. Be sure that the letters present you in the best light and are consistent with how you describe yourself in your résumé and interviews.

▪ When Should You Submit Your Letters of Recommendation?

There is no hard-and-fast rule on when to give a prospective employer your letters of recommendation. Since they are not routinely requested in the way that a résumé or job application is, you'll have to use your best judgment. If your letters are relevant to the job you're applying for and they are extremely positive, you may want to include them with your résumé and cover letter. If you think your résumé and cover letter are strong enough to stand alone, then wait until the interview to present them or until the prospective employer requests them. Treat your letters as one more job-hunting tool.

CARLA MORAN

5585 Kensington Way
Brooklyn, NY 98921
(404) 555-7534

April 12, 2000

Mr. Kevin Lorita
Vice President, Human Resources
Sundown Corporation
338 Orleans Lane
Brooklyn, NY 98921

Dear Kevin:

As you know, I will be graduating in June and am seeking full-time employment as a human resources representative back in my hometown of Charlotte, South Carolina. I would greatly appreciate it if you could write a letter of recommendation for me regarding my work in your department as a human resources coordinator during the last two years.

I have taken the liberty of drafting a letter to help expedite the process. Feel free to edit the letter or write one of your own. Then please return the final draft to me on company letter-head by April 24, 2000, if at all possible.

Thank you in advance. I will stay in touch and keep you apprised of my job search.

Sincerely,

Carla Moran

Carla Moran

Enclosure

Cover Letter to Request a Letter of Recommendation

Sundown Corporation
338 Orleans Lane
Brooklyn, NY 98921
(404) 555-1121

April 20, 2000

To Whom It May Concern:

Carla Moran worked as a human resources coordinator for two years in my department at Sundown Corporation. During that time, Carla had diverse responsibilities. She reviewed résumés to identify qualified employment candidates, conducted preliminary applicant interviews, and documented hiring-firing policy decisions for distribution to Sundown's various department supervisors.

Carla is bright, articulate, and hard working. Her enthusiasm for the job comes through in all she does. She has a positive attitude that makes her a pleasure to work with and is one of the reasons she was so well liked by her coworkers.

I highly recommend Carla for any job she is considering in the Human Resources field. She would be an asset to any employer. If you have further questions about Carla, please do not hesitate to contact me at (404) 555-1121, ext. 200.

Sincerely,

Kevin Lorita
Vice President, Human Resources

Letter of Recommendation Proposed by the Job Hunter

Filling Out
Job Applications

The Application Form

Many companies require a completed application form as well as a résumé before they will interview you. Although this small step in your job hunt isn't difficult, you must avoid several mistakes that will eliminate your application from the pile.

1. **Write in pen.** Pencil smudges look unprofessional. Bring a pen with you to appear more prepared.

2. **Print clearly.** Imagine the frustration of an employer who is interested in your application but cannot decipher your name or phone number.

3. **Use one lettering style.** You can print or use script, whichever is your neater penmanship, but be sure to stick with your choice throughout the application.

4. **Complete every line.** If a section is not applicable, write "n/a" or draw a line through the answer space. Check the side and top or bottom margins and both sides of the paper for questions you might have missed.

5. **Know your work history.** Bring with you, on an index card, the names, addresses, and phone numbers of all your former employers, plus a list of people to contact for information about you. If your experience is limited, it is perfectly acceptable to also include names of people for whom you've done odd jobs, such as yard work or baby-sitting.

6. **Choose references carefully.** Before you begin filling out job applications, it is a good idea to call or write to ask permission to use someone's name as a reference and to remind that person of your current career goals. Do not list a person if you have the least bit of doubt about getting a good reference. You may not have much space on the form, but an ideal mix would be two to three professional references who could discuss the quality of your work and one to two personal references (not relatives) who could discuss your character.

7. **Be careful when writing salary requirements.** If possible, avoid committing yourself to a specific number. An amount that is too high could eliminate you, and an amount that is too low could cost you if you're hired. If you must write a desired salary, research the going rate in your field and write a salary range that would be acceptable to you.

8. **Use only recognizable abbreviations.** This will help make your application as easy to read as possible.

9. **Be neat.** Remember that the attention you show to your application reflects how you will perform at work. Messy scratch-outs and missed questions will leave a bad impression.

10. **Be courteous to everyone you meet at the job location.** Many people who go to fill out applications dress sloppily. They assume that since the applica-

tion visit isn't a formal interview, they can be casual, rude, or unprepared. Remember that your first contact with an employer creates a strong impression. Dress as you would for the job interview. Also, remember to be friendly and courteous even to those whom you might consider "unimportant," such as clerks and secretaries. These people may have input in the hiring decision and could end up being your coworkers.

11. **Proofread.** In the rush of job hunting, it is easy to become nervous and careless. Show the employer that you pay attention to detail by handing in an application that represents a job well done.

■ Typical Application Questions

Although every job application form is a little different, there are some questions that are fairly common. Review the following list to better prepare your answers:

1. **Name.** Follow instructions in this blank. Applications often require you to place your last name first and to include your middle initial.

2. **Address.** Give your entire address, including ZIP code.

3. **Phone number.** Be sure that the phone you list will always be answered, even if only by an answering machine.

4. **Social Security number.** Often your Social Security number becomes your employee identification number, which companies then use to input and retrieve your file from their system.

5. **In case of emergency.** Name a person who can be reached during your work hours and who can respond quickly to an emergency situation, preferably someone local and with their own transportation.

6. **Citizenship.** The employer wants to know if you are a U.S. citizen or an alien who has a legal right to hold the job for which you are applying.

7. **Position applying for.** Be as specific as possible in naming the type of job you seek. Use the correct title of the job if you know it.

8. **Salary desired.** Unless you know the exact salary being offered for the job you want, you would do better to give a range that will leave you some room for negotiation. You may also use terms such as "to be discussed" or "negotiable" if you think it would be to your benefit to avoid listing a figure.

9. **Date available.** Give the soonest possible date you could begin a job. If you are currently unemployed, you should put "immediately." If you have a job, plan to give at least two weeks' notice to your current employer.

10. **Education.** List high school, college, graduate school, and any specialized courses or certifications you've completed.

11. **Work experience.** You should have this information prepared before you begin filling out the application form. You'll need to include the names of previous employers and their addresses and phone numbers as well as your job title, dates of employment, and supervisor's name. You may also be asked your reason for leaving a former job. Present your response in a positive light, for example, "Was ready for new challenges and additional responsibility."

12. **Military service.** List your military experience or write "n/a" for "not applicable."

13. **Have you ever been convicted of a crime?** Answer honestly. Many employers routinely check for criminal records. If the employer hires you and then learns you lied, you will be fired.

14. **Hobbies or interests.** Use this area to call attention to any specific interests you have that might make you a more valuable employee or demonstrate you have a well-rounded personality.

15. **Foreign language ability.** List the languages besides English that you know. You may also be asked to assess your proficiency in reading, writing, and speaking a foreign language.

16. **References.** List previous employers, teachers, or other professional references. Be prepared to provide their phone numbers and addresses. Do not use relatives. Character references need to have known you for at least two years.

17. **Signature and date.** Important! Your signature and date confirm that you have, to the best of your knowledge, completed the questions accurately. An application is not considered valid unless it is signed and dated.

18. **For personnel use only.** Check out this section to get a hint about the kinds of information the prospective employer will seek in your interview.

EXERCISE

On the following pages is a sample employment application. Fill it out for practice and to create a master document with all your relevant information. Refer to it when completing actual employment applications.

APPLICATION FOR EMPLOYMENT

PRE-EMPLOYMENT QUESTIONNAIRE
EQUAL OPPORTUNITY EMPLOYER

PERSONAL INFORMATION

DATE _____

NAME (LAST NAME FIRST)		SOCIAL SECURITY NO.

PRESENT ADDRESS	CITY	STATE	ZIP CODE

PERMANENT ADDRESS	CITY	STATE	ZIP CODE

PHONE NO. ( )	REFERRED BY

EMPLOYMENT DESIRED

POSITION	DATE YOU CAN START	SALARY DESIRED

ARE YOU EMPLOYED? ☐ YES ☐ NO	IF SO, MAY WE INQUIRE OF YOUR PRESENT EMPLOYER? ☐ YES ☐ NO

EVER APPLIED TO THIS COMPANY BEFORE? ☐ YES ☐ NO	WHERE?	WHEN?

EDUCATION HISTORY

	NAME & LOCATION OF SCHOOL	YEARS ATTENDED	DID YOU GRADUATE?	SUBJECTS STUDIED
GRAMMAR SCHOOL				
HIGH SCHOOL				
COLLEGE				
TRADE, BUSINESS OR CORRESPONDENCE SCHOOL				

GENERAL INFORMATION

SUBJECTS OF SPECIAL STUDY/RESEARCH WORK OR SPECIAL TRAINING/SKILLS

U.S. MILITARY OR NAVAL SERVICE	RANK

FORMER EMPLOYERS (LIST BELOW LAST FOUR EMPLOYERS, STARTING WITH LAST ONE FIRST)

DATE MONTH AND YEAR	NAME & ADDRESS OF EMPLOYER	SALARY	POSITION	REASON FOR LEAVING
FROM / TO				
FROM / TO				
FROM / TO				
FROM / TO				

APPLICATION FOR EMPLOYMENT

CONTINUED ON OTHER SIDE

REFERENCES GIVE BELOW THE NAMES OF THREE PERSONS NOT RELATED TO YOU, WHOM YOU HAVE KNOWN AT LEAST ONE YEAR.

NAME	ADDRESS	BUSINESS	YEARS KNOWN

AUTHORIZATION

"I certify that the facts contained in this application are true and complete to the best of my knowledge and understand that, if employed, falsified statements on this application shall be grounds for dismissal.

I authorize investigation of all statements contained herein and the references and employers listed above to give you any and all information concerning my previous employment and any pertinent information they may have, personal or otherwise, and release the company from all liability for any damage that may result from utilization of such information.

I also understand and agree that no representative of the company has any authority to enter into any agreement for employment for any specified period of time, or to make any agreement contrary to the forego-ing, unless it is in writing and signed by an authorized company representative."

DATE_____ SIGNATURE _____

INTERVIEWED BY _____ DATE _____

———————————— DO NOT WRITE BELOW THIS LINE ————————————

REMARKS

NEATNESS		CHARACTER		
PERSONALITY		ABILITY		
HIRED	FOR DEPT.	POSITION	WILL REPORT	SALARY WAGES

APPROVED: 1. _____ 2. _____ 3. _____
　　　　　　 EMPLOYMENT MANAGER 　　　 DEPARTMENT HEAD 　　　 GENERAL MANAGER

CHAPTER

10

Interviewing

Prepare for the Interview

Many people are unprepared for interviewing and therefore are more nervous than they have to be. Think of the interview as a three-step process, and plan the execution of each step. Remember that you have only a short time to convey your experience, potential, and personality. As you go through the interview process, envision the person with whom you'll be interviewing. Remember that this individual will likely be of a different generation or background. Keep in mind that person may have conservative expectations about your dress and conduct. Dress and act not as if you were with one of your peers, but as someone who may hold you to a higher standard.

Prepare for the different types of interviewers that you may encounter. Often, job applicants are interviewed first by a human resources manager, then by a department manager or direct supervisor. Sometimes two or three of these people conduct the interview together. As a job hunter, your ideal is to get to the person to whom you'd be reporting. Remember that human resources managers often function as "screeners," whose primary role is to weed people out. Some human resources people have only a general knowledge of the available position and are reluctant to describe the people with whom you'd be working most closely. Your goal is to either bypass the human resources department or be impressive enough to make it to the next step: your future supervisor.

Use these guidelines to prepare for the interview, and review it frequently during your job search:

- **Before the Interview**

    1. Dress properly (to ensure that the interviewer remembers you, not your clothes).

    2. Be on time.

    3. Research the organization—what it does and its projects, future plans, size, and problems. Start with the company's web site and annual report.

    4. Be prepared to ask questions—you're interviewing the employer, too!

    5. Bring résumés and examples of past performance.

    6. Practice your responses.

        a. Role-play interviewing with a friend.

        b. Think through your answers aloud while you're driving or in front of the mirror at home.

        c. Paraphrase. To show you're a good listener, practice rephrasing in your own words the information given by the interviewer in your role-playing exercise.

- **During the Interview**

  1. Create a positive, initial greeting: Give a firm handshake and display a positive attitude.

  2. Be truthful, but never put yourself down.

  3. Speak distinctly.

  4. Help the interviewer.

     a. Explain your experiences and skills.

     b. Relate your experiences and skills to the job for which you're interviewing.

  5. Don't be too serious or too humorous.

  6. Listen carefully and make good eye contact.

  7. Be concise.

  8. Do not oversell yourself.

- **After the Interview** (often neglected but vital steps)

  1. Write down information and discussion points about the organization and the job.

  2. Evaluate your interview; determine how to improve your next one.

  3. Write follow-up letters.

  4. Follow up with phone calls to determine the status of the hiring decision.

■ Types of Interviews

KEY POINT

Not all interviews are alike. Knowing about and preparing for the different types of interviews can prevent surprises. With proper preparation you'll be able to demonstrate your skills and convey your personality effectively in any type of interview.

Behavioral or situational interviews.   An increasingly popular type of interview, the behavioral or situational interview is based on the premise that your past performance is the best predictor of your future performance. The interviewer will typically ask very specific, probing questions to tease out your behaviors in the past. The candidate's job is to briefly and specifically explain past situations, actions taken, and results achieved.

Board interviews.   The candidate may meet with several interviewers in a more formal setting. These interviews are most often used for hiring at the corporate level, where several people may want to be directly involved in the decision process. Board interviews require special preparation and forethought.

Directed interviews. These follow a definite set of questions. You may notice that the interviewer has a checklist. Directed interviews are usually used to pre-screen applicants for another interview.

Group interviews. An interviewer may ask the job candidate to work with others on a particular task or topic. Observers note your leadership abilities and skill at working as part of a team. Group interviews require special preparation and forethought.

Informational interviews. (See the section on informational interviews on page 70.) Some job hunters use this type of interview to gain information from a person who works in a field of interest to them. This is the only type of interview in which the candidate does not ask for a job at the end of the session.

Lunch or dinner interviews. Held in a more casual setting, the lunch or dinner interview allows the interviewer and applicant a chance to more easily develop a rapport. Follow the host's lead in ordering food and in business etiquette while remembering that all other interview rules still apply.

Nondirected interviews. Interviews that are less structured and less formal are often used in more informal work places. They may allow you more room for expression. The questions asked tend to be open-ended and are very spontaneous.

Stress interviews. Some interviews are designed to see how well a job candidate holds up under pressure. If the position you're applying for involves a great deal of stress, don't be surprised to encounter a high-pressure interviewer. Even interviewers for nonstressful jobs may want to try to shake your poise by using rapid-fire or tricky questions. Recognize this type of interview for what it is—a test. (Consider whether or not you'd feel comfortable working for an employer who uses this type of interview.)

Telephone interviews. This type of interview may use a combination of different interviewing techniques. For example, you may be interviewed by one person or a group. Telephone interviews are typically used to screen out applicants, although they may also be used as a follow-up to an earlier conversation. The job hunter's primary goal when faced with this type of interview is to seek a face-to-face meeting. (See page 130 for more on telephone interviews.)

EXERCISE

EXERCISE
Preparation Worksheet

By thinking through your skills, you will be better prepared to explain them to the interviewer and relate them to the position you want.

Past Job, Hobby, or Volunteer Work	**Skill I Learned/Value to Employer**
1. _____	1. _____
2. _____	2. _____
3. _____	3. _____
4. _____	4. _____
5. _____	5. _____

Here is an alternative way to organize your thoughts before an interview:

My Strongest Skills	**Where I Developed Them/Examples**
1. _____	1. _____
2. _____	2. _____
3. _____	3. _____
4. _____	4. _____
5. _____	5. _____

Create a Good First Impression

KEY POINT

Studies have shown that people form an opinion of someone they meet in the first two to four minutes. For that reason, it is vital that you pay attention to detail to create the best first impression you can. Some factors that will affect the impression you make are your age, sex, appearance (hair, clothes, hygiene, jewelry, make-up), movement, mannerisms, personal space, and manner of speaking. Good manners also play an important role.

■ Rules of Business Etiquette

To help enhance your chances of making a favorable impression, follow these basic rules:

1.   Arrive on time.

2.   Introduce yourself politely to the receptionist and state the first and last name of the individual whom you are to see.

3.   If the receptionist offers, you may accept coffee or tea, but be sure you won't have trouble juggling the cup and your résumé materials when you have to shake hands with the interviewer. It might be best to politely pass on the offer.

4.   If you accept a soft drink from the receptionist or your interviewer, be sure to pour it into a cup, if available, rather than drinking from the can.

5.   Do not chew gum.

6.   Do not smoke. It is also best not to smoke just before an interview, as many people find the residual smell offensive.

7.   Introduce yourself to the interviewer by clearly stating both your first and last name. Make eye contact and smile.

8.   Say "It's nice to meet you" in your initial greeting.

9.   Address the interviewer as Mr. _____ or Ms. _____ unless you are asked to do otherwise. Don't assume that if the interviewer calls you by your first name you are both on a first-name basis.

10.   Be willing to make a bit of small talk, possibly about the weather, the traffic on the way to the interview, or about the interviewer's good directions that got you there.

11.   After the interviewer has led you from the reception area to an office or conference room to talk further, do not take a seat until the interviewer motions you to a particular place.

12.   Sit straight and relatively still. Avoid distracting wiggling or jiggling of your hands or legs.

13.   Fold your hands in your lap comfortably or on top of your résumé materials. Do not cross your arms over your chest (it will make you appear disagreeable) or spread them across the back of the chair or couch (it will make you appear too relaxed, lazy, or uninterested).

14.   Be attentive when the interviewer speaks. Avoid interrupting, even if the interviewer does most of the talking. Maintain good eye contact with the interviewer.

15.   Don't hesitate to ask for clarification if you don't understand something.

16. Be positive and upbeat in your remarks.

17. Avoid complaining about a previous job or employer. Whether or not your remarks are true, you won't appear professional if you harp on these subjects.

18. Avoid criticizing, contradicting, or disagreeing with the interviewer.

19. If you are offered a tour of the facility, the interviewer will indicate whether you are to walk ahead or to follow. Women should know that male interviewers may often encourage them to pass through doorways first.

20. At the end of the meeting, thank the interviewer for his or her time and extend your hand for a strong parting handshake. Don't forget to smile and make eye contact one last time.

■ Dress to Impress

As a job hunter, you need to keep in mind that most people quickly form a first and lasting impression of you. Keep your dress understated, conservative, and neat. If you're unsure about what to wear, a good rule of thumb is to dress slightly better than you would to report to the job every day. For example, at some work places blue jeans are perfectly acceptable garb; you could wear casual slacks to a job interview with such an organization.

How do you determine the dress code in your intended work place? Research. Ask around. If it's a public place, such as a bank or restaurant, drop by and observe. If you're still unsure, a suit in a dark or neutral color is almost always a good choice. Wear something you've worn at least once before, just to be certain that you'll feel comfortable and confident. Of course, avoid anything that looks visibly worn, torn, or wrinkled.

Here are some other details that can leave an interviewer with a poor impression.

Women should avoid:

- Hair that is too styled, overteased, or overmoussed. Keep hair pulled back and conservatively styled.

- Dangly earrings, or too many earrings, rings, necklaces, or bracelets.

- Too much make-up or perfume. Too little is always better than too much.

- Low-cut or unbuttoned blouses or any sign of an undergarment (straps or anything that would show through a sheer blouse or skirt). Going braless is a definite no-no.

- Patterned nylons. Plain, sheer hose are best.

- Tight, short, or leather or suede skirts.

- Trendy or faddish accessories such as exposed tattoos and body piercings.

- Lots of ruffles, bows, or fringe. Remember that you want to appear businesslike and professional.

- Very high heels, glittery, silver or gold shoes, or open-toed shoes.

If obtaining professional clothes is a financial impossibility for you, go to Dress For Success at www.dressforsuccess.org. This nonprofit organization helps low-income women make tailored transitions into the work force by providing donated suits to job hunters.

Men should avoid:

- Long, unkempt hair. Wear it short or tie it back and keep it conservatively styled.

- Earrings, bracelets, pinkie rings, or similar jewelry.

- Too much aftershave or cologne.

- Unbuttoned shirts.

- T-shirts or patterned T-shirts under dress shirts.

- White socks or socks that clash with slacks. Also avoid brown shoes with black slacks or vice versa.

- Sheer white slacks.

- Novelty ties or leather ties.

- Sneakers or sandals.

- Exposed tattoos or body piercings.

It's often helpful to try a "dress rehearsal" the evening before a job interview. First, you'll have an opportunity to find missing buttons or fallen hems while you can still remedy them. Second, you can ask the opinion of a good friend or relative. Finally, you'll have the opportunity to see your put-together, professional self and to gain confidence and poise for the interview.

EXERCISE

Choose a day to wear your interview clothes to class. Ask your classmates or instructor for feedback. Can they guess your career field or desired position? What did they notice first? Solicit constructive criticism, both positive and negative. Make notes for future interviews.

■ Presenting Yourself on the Telephone

Your initial phone call to a potential employer can often mean the difference between getting an interview and being overlooked as a candidate for a job.

Whenever your first contact with an employer is by telephone, always be sure to be courteous to whomever answers the phone. Support staff are often the people who decide whether calls should be put through, and in today's leaner, customer-service-oriented companies, it is not uncommon for supervisors themselves to answer the phone.

One trick for calling difficult-to-reach executives is to try early in the morning or after 5:00 P.M. These are typically hours when managers are at work but their secretaries are not, so the person you wish to speak to is more likely to answer. In general, it's best to make calls in the morning when people are alert and not yet immersed in the day's events.

KEY POINT

1. The first rule of telephone etiquette is to be prepared. Know whom you want to speak to and what you want to say. You may want to practice your presentation, but try not to sound too rehearsed when you finally place your call. Make sure you clear away any distractions. Crying children in the background or television or kitchen noise will detract from your professionalism. Set a goal for the phone call, such as to obtain an interview appointment or establish an initial contact.

2. Ask politely but authoritatively for the person you want to reach. If you sound hesitant or unsure of yourself, you may have more difficulty getting past the secretary. If you were referred by a mutual contact, give that person's name to the secretary to help ensure that your call is put through.

3. If the secretary tells you that the person you wish to reach is unavailable, offer to call back. Often, executives won't return unsolicited calls from job hunters. Ask the secretary to recommend a good time for you to try again. After a few tries, you might try leaving a message. State your first and last name, the reason you're calling, your phone number, and the best time to reach you. Don't be personally insulted if your call is not returned. This is often standard operating procedure. By being politely persistent and calling again, your efforts may eventually be rewarded.

When you do eventually get through to the person you want, express a quick greeting, identify yourself using both your first and last name, and briefly state why you're calling. Every conversation will differ, of course, so you'll need to vary your approach. In an ideal situation, you'll have a receptive listener on the other end of the line. Begin to highlight your assets, explaining how your skills match the company's needs. Briefly mention some of your successes or specific accomplishments at a previous job or in school. Pause when appropriate to allow the person to provide feedback and ask questions.

Most likely you will be aiming for an in-person meeting, so you needn't insist on an extensive telephone interview. Hiring decisions are rarely, if ever, made over the phone. Ask for an interview by saying something like: "I've enjoyed speaking with you. Is there a convenient time we could get together and talk further in person?" If the person suggests you first send in your résumé, agree to put one in the mail and attempt again to set up a time for a follow-up meeting. If the response is still negative, thank the individual for talking with you. Explain that you will send the résumé and will follow up with another call in a week or so, after he or she has had time to review it.

KEY POINT

Make sure you keep a list of whom you've called, when you called, and what the next action is to be. Calling back when you say you will is an easy way of demonstrating to an employer that you are serious about a position and that you are dependable.

■ The Telephone Interview

Whereas you may use the telephone to try to obtain an interview, some employers will use it to do the actual interview, or at least have a preliminary "meeting." Usually, phone interviews happen in one of three ways:

1. You cold-call the prospective employer to get information about job availability, and the employer begins asking you interview questions immediately because you aroused his or her interest.

2. A company calls you unexpectedly as a response to a letter and/or résumé you sent.

3. You or a placement agency have set up a specific time for a telephone interview.

No matter how the interview comes about, the bottom line is the same—a prospective employer is interested in you. It's vital that you seize the opportunity to get to the next step, an in-person meeting. Therefore, the telephone interview becomes a trial run for the real thing.

Being effective in a telephone interview, as in a face-to-face meeting, takes preparation. Since you never know when a company might call you once you've got your networking process under way, you should keep a file of companies you've contacted next to the phone. Be sure the file is organized (alphabetical order by company name usually works best) so that you can quickly locate a copy of the materials you sent the caller and also any research you may have done about the company.

The most important point to remember is that the phone interview is usually a weeding-out process. The interviewer is listening for any indication that you might *not* be the right person for the job and that it would be a waste of time to arrange a face-to-face meeting. Here are some tips to help you succeed in a phone interview:

1. **Take a surprise call in stride.** Even though the call may come at the most inopportune time, try to sound pleased, friendly, and collected.

2. **Let the interviewer do most of the talking.** Try to keep your answers to questions brief and to the point. Rambling on the phone will bore the interviewer. However, try to avoid giving yes or no answers that don't provide information about your abilities.

3. **Don't hesitate to ask some of your own questions.** This is also your opportunity to learn a little bit more about the company and the position in question. What information you gain will help you decide if you're interested in the job and, if so, will prove useful to you in preparing for an in-person interview. Under no circumstances, though, should you ask about money or vacation time. It would be premature and inappropriate. Your focus should be on the responsibilities of the position.

4. **Speak clearly into the telephone.** Don't eat, drink, or smoke while on the phone. Turn down any background music and eliminate other background noises as best as possible.

5. **Take notes of your conversation.** Keep pen and paper close to the phone at all times just for this reason. You'll want to jot down any relevant information the interviewer gives you about the position. You may also need to write down a meeting time and directions for your in-person interview.

6. **Be sure to get a name and phone number.** If you have been invited to meet with the interviewer, write down his or her name and phone number so that you can make contact should you have to change the appointment for any reason.

7. **Anticipate dialogue.** Rehearse possible questions and your responses. Create cue cards as prompts.

8. **Avoid salary issues.** If pressed, present a wide salary range that is acceptable to you, noting that you do not yet know enough about the specific position or its demands.

9. **Try to reschedule.** Surprise interviews are difficult even for the most seasoned job hunter. See if you can make an appointment for another time when you can prepare your notes and create a calm and productive interview setting.

10. **Push for a face-to-face interview.** Ask, "May we discuss this further next Tuesday afternoon?"

11. **Extend thanks.** Close the conversation with appreciation for the caller's interest.

Remember that your single objective at this point is to sell yourself such that the interviewer requests an in-person meeting. It is unlikely you will ever be offered a position after only a phone interview. If the interviewer does not offer you a face-to-face meeting, take the initiative to ask for one. At that point, you have nothing to lose.

DIVE IN

It is difficult to evaluate an opportunity over the phone. Even if the job doesn't sound right, go to the interview. It will give you practice. Also, the job may sound better when you get all the facts. You might even learn of a more suitable position elsewhere within the company when you have your in-person meeting.

How to Handle Interview Stress

Many people consider a job interview one of life's most stressful events. Some become so overwhelmed that they sabotage their own success. If you feel overly threatened by a job interview, try the exercises described in the following sections.

■ Put Things into Perspective

Some people place so much importance on each interview that the pressure to succeed becomes crippling. When you catch yourself thinking terrifying thoughts that start with the word *if,* stop and redirect yourself. "If" thoughts have a tendency to pile up and weigh you down.

For example, a nonproductive train of thought might proceed this way: "*If* I don't do well at this interview, I'll be so disappointed. I'll never have the confidence to do well at another interview" or "*If* I don't land this job, my parents (spouse, friends) will think I'm such a failure. How will I pay for the rent (car, mortgage)?" These thoughts are self-defeating and negative. They also tend to focus on the future, which you can't control, at the expense of the present, which you can control.

Instead of terrorizing yourself with "what *ifs*," be your own best friend. Say nothing to yourself that you wouldn't say to a good friend to whom you were trying to lend confidence. Say everything to yourself that you'd say to a friend who needed a little extra support going into a stressful situation.

Instead of thinking:	*Tell yourself:*
What *if* I become tongue-tied during the interview and ruin my chances?	Of course it's natural for me to feel nervous at first, but I'm sure I'll relax and do fine.

EXERCISE

EXERCISE   In the space below, write down a few positive, calming, and confidence-producing thoughts. (If you have trouble doing this, think of things you would say to a good friend.)

Positive Statements

1. _____

_____

2. _____

_____

3. _____

_____

If you need to, read these over just before you go to the interview. After all, why should you give yourself any less support and respect than you would your best friend?

■ Sweaty Palms Are Not a Crime

Sometimes, even though you can calm your stressful thoughts, your body will not cooperate. Sweaty palms, a nervous stomach, and a dry mouth are symptoms occasionally felt by nervous job hunters everywhere. Don't let this physical discomfort throw you. Try a few relaxation techniques:

1. Use nature's original relaxation device: the sigh. Allow yourself a few huge sighs and notice how tension leaves your body.

2. Focus on your breathing. Even while sitting in a waiting room, you can take long, slow, deep breaths. If you have the opportunity, close your eyes, sit comfortably, and imagine that your breath has a color. In your mind's eye, watch for a few minutes as you breathe in and out of your nose. The resulting deep breaths will prevent you from focusing on nervous thoughts while relaxing your muscles and oxygenating your brain. (Try it now and see.)

3. Slowly tense and release each muscle group in your body sequentially. Start with your toes and work up to your head. Some people also imagine their body as a vessel filled with warm sunshine.

Bookstores and libraries offer many books on ways to relax. If you need to, do some research to find a few tricks that work for you.

Finally, remember that stress is not all bad. Each of us needs a little stress to be productive. Think of the adrenaline as an asset. Why not use this extra zip to project more energy, think clearly, and speak distinctly? Focus on ways to let stress work *for* you and not *against* you.

INTERNET If you think you need additional help in managing your stress, visit the following web sites: International Stress Management Association, at www.stress-management-isma.org; Mind Tools: How to Master Stress, at www.mindtools.com/smpage.html; Job Stress Help, at www.jobstresshelp.com; Stress Free Net, at www.stressfree.com; and Townsend International, at www.gday-mate.com.

Do You Have Interview Anxiety?

	Never	Sometimes	Always
Before an interview:			
I have trouble sleeping the night before.	❑	❑	❑
I get a headache.	❑	❑	❑
I get a stomachache.	❑	❑	❑
I lose my appetite.	❑	❑	❑
My palms sweat.	❑	❑	❑
I have canceled an interview because of panic.	❑	❑	❑
In an interview:			
My hands shake.	❑	❑	❑
I have trouble remembering things.	❑	❑	❑
My mind keeps going blank.	❑	❑	❑
I tap my hands or feet constantly.	❑	❑	❑
I crack my knuckles frequently.	❑	❑	❑
I can't think clearly.	❑	❑	❑
I can't wait to get out of the room.	❑	❑	❑
I feel nervous and jittery.	❑	❑	❑
I worry that I'm doing poorly.	❑	❑	❑
I have a hard time understanding directions.	❑	❑	❑
I can't remember things I said.	❑	❑	❑
I feel like crying.	❑	❑	❑
I feel exhausted.	❑	❑	❑

Tally your check marks. If you have more than five checks in the "Sometimes" or "Always" columns, plan a strategy for extra interview practice.

■ Hide Your Nervousness

All interviewers expect interviewees to be at least a little nervous when they come in, but you don't want your nervous actions to detract from your appearance and the impression you make. By becoming aware of the nervous signals you unconsciously give off, you'll be able to eliminate them and have better interviews. See if you find yourself exhibiting any of these behaviors:

❏ Playing with your hair

❏ Wringing your hands

❏ Cracking your knuckles

❏ Clearing your throat

❏ Tugging at your ear

❏ Playing with your jewelry

❏ Touching your neck

❏ Picking or pinching your skin

❏ Jingling money in your pocket

❏ Covering your mouth with your hands when you speak

❏ Tapping your hands, feet, or pen

❏ Swiveling in your chair

EXERCISE

Now do a mock interview with a friend while a silent third person looks on out of your line of vision. (Better yet, videotape yourself!) Have the observer take notes, listing any nervous signals you display.

Once you've identified the ways in which your anxiety manifests itself, you can focus on eliminating these tendencies, continuing to practice your interview skills at home. However, the best remedy is simply doing as many interviews as you can, even for jobs in which you may not be that interested. The real-world practice you'll receive from these interviews will enable you to perfect your presentation, gain self-confidence, and eventually minimize, if not altogether eliminate, your feelings of anxiety.

Questions Asked in Job Interviews

■ Questions an Interviewer Might Ask You

As always, practice makes perfect. Look at the following list of questions and answer them aloud. This exercise will lessen the chances that you'll be caught off-guard in an actual interview.

1. Tell me about yourself.

2. What is your grade point average?

3. What is your major?

4. What courses do you enjoy in college?

5. What courses don't you enjoy?

6. What do you know about our organization?

7. What can you do for us? Why should we hire you?

8. What qualifications do you have that make you feel you will be successful in your field?

9. How did you hear about this position?

10. What types of jobs have you had in the past? What did you learn?

11. What have you learned from the jobs you've held?

12. Have you participated in any volunteer or community work? What did you learn there?

13. How do you feel about routine work?

14. What are your future vocational plans?

15. If you could write your own ticket, what would be your dream job?

16. Are you willing to travel?

17. What have you done that shows initiative and willingness to work?

18. Are you involved in any extracurricular activities?

19. Do you hold any positions of leadership at school?

20. What are your special skills, and where did you acquire them?

21. Have you had any special accomplishments in your lifetime that you are particularly proud of?

22. Why did you leave your most recent job?

23. Do you have any geographical restrictions or preferences?

24. How do you spend your spare time? What are your hobbies?

25. What percentage of your college expenses did you earn? How?

26. What do you consider your strengths? Your weaknesses?

27. What books have you read recently?

28. If you were fired from a previous job, what was the reason?

29. Discuss five major accomplishments.

30. When can you start work?

31. When can you visit our headquarters for further interviews?

32. What kind of boss would you like?

33. If you could spend a day with someone you've known or known of, who would it be?

34. What personality characteristics seem to rub you the wrong way?

35. Define *cooperation*.

36. How do you show your anger? What type of things make you angry?

37. What activities have you ever quit?

38. Have you ever experienced discrimination yourself?

39. What does "9 to 5" mean to you?

40. With what type of person do you spend the majority of your time?

Remember that "questions" come in many forms. You may be asked to perform a task during the interview. This task could be anything from composing a letter to working on a project. Be prepared to demonstrate your expertise.

EXERCISE

Identifying Your Interests

As several of the above sample questions indicate, many employers will ask you how you spend your spare time. Although this information may not seem directly relevant to a particular job, it can give the employer additional insight into your personality and your preferences.

Take time to identify your interests before going to an interview. Below, list the five interests or hobbies that you pursue most frequently, and briefly describe your participation. Your answers may range from sports activities to volunteer work to club memberships. In an actual interview, you may wish to avoid mentioning any political or religious affiliations that could count against you. Use your best judgment in making that decision.

Your Interests

1. _____

2. _____

3. _____

4. _____

_____

5. _____

_____

■ Illegal Interview Questions

There are some things an interviewer shouldn't ask, usually information of a personal nature; however, it is not uncommon to be asked an illegal question. Usually, interviewers ask one of these questions not out of malice but out of simple ignorance—they are unaware of the law. Although laws vary from state to state, companies should not ask questions or make comments about your sex, marital status, race, color, religion, housing, physical data, or disabilities.

A smart job hunter is aware of the questions that he or she is not obligated to answer and knows the options when responding. Basically, you have three choices when confronted with an illegal question:

1. Answer the question and ignore the fact that it is not legal.

2. Ask, "I wonder why you would ask that question?" Then, upon hearing the interviewer's response, decide whether or not to answer.

3. Contact the nearest Equal Employment Office. However, be aware that although you may have a legitimate claim, it is difficult to prove you have been the victim of discrimination. Hence, this may not be your best option.

Whichever option you choose, pause to consider whether you'd like to work for an employer who is so interested in your personal life. (After you are hired, of course, your company may need personal information, such as your marital status and the names and ages of your children for insurance purposes.)

Seemingly illegal questions are legitimate if they are related to genuine job requirements. For example, it is perfectly acceptable for a shipping company to inquire into your physical stature if your job would require heavy lifting. It would also be appropriate for a company to ask your age if the position required the handling of liquor.

■ Questions to Ask an Interviewer

Remember that you are interviewing prospective employers at the same time that they are interviewing you. Ask questions that will help you determine whether the position meets your skills, desires, and career goals. Asking intelligent questions will make you appear interested and enthusiastic to the interviewer. Here, then, are some suggested questions:

1. Tell me about the nature of the position. What are the specific duties and responsibilities? Is a written job description available?

2. What type of training can I expect in the first six months? Down the road?

3. Are there any travel requirements?

4. To whom would I report? Can you tell me something about his or her background?

5. Is this a newly created position? If not, who was the last person to occupy this position, and what is he or she doing now?

6. Does this organization promote activities that aid in professional growth, such as participation in business societies or seminars?

7. How long has the company been in business? Tell me about the company's history.

8. What types of customers does it service? What types of products does it sell?

9. What are the company's plans for the future?

10. What are the future possibilities for promotion within the company?

11. Can I provide you with any other information about myself?

12. What is the next step in the decision process? When will a final decision be made regarding the position?

It's best not to inquire about salary during the first interview. With careful research, you should have an idea of the salary range of the position. In addition, you will want to demonstrate that you are more interested in the company and the position than the money, so delay your questions about salary, benefits, and perks until the second interview or until the company makes you a job offer.

You've Got Personality

KEY POINT

Despite the formality of the interview process, the hidden agenda for most interviewers is to get to know you. Of course, although your education and skills are deciding factors, how an interviewer perceives your personality will help him or her decide whether you have the right chemistry for the job. Don't be afraid to let your personality shine through.

To determine your "personality type," the interviewer searches for personal profile keys in your answers to the questions. Below are some of the personality traits interviewers look for the most.

▓ Personal Profile Keys

- **Drive.** People who are goal oriented are always striving to do better. They especially like to get tasks accomplished.

- **Motivation.** Enthusiasm and energy go a long way toward success. Employers recognize that a motivated person accepts challenges and is willing to give that little bit extra on the job.

- **Communication skills.** No matter the company or type of business, the ability to communicate effectively both orally and in writing is vital.

- **Chemistry.** Like the real world, getting along with others at work is extremely important. Employers appreciate team players, confident individuals, and generally happy people.

- **Energy.** Energetic people get the job done and help energize those around them. They can be a very positive influence in the work environment.

- **Determination.** The employer wants someone who will finish a project when started, solve problems, and take on challenges.

- **Confidence.** A confident employee is proud of his or her accomplishments without being arrogant. Confident people are often very effective in doing their job.

■ Professional Profile Keys

- **Reliability.** Management wants to be sure they can count on you to get the job done, no matter how challenging. In the real world, only performance counts.

- **Honesty.** Employers want someone whom they can trust and who has personal integrity.

- **Pride.** People who take pride in their work always do a good job. They pay attention to details and seek to do things "right," not just "good enough."

- **Dedication.** The best employees are those who make the effort to see a task through to completion. Their commitment to the job makes them valuable assets.

- **Analytical skills.** A person who is able to evaluate a situation, troubleshoot a problem, and take appropriate action makes a good employee.

- **Listening skills.** People who listen show they care. They value others' opinions and learn from those around them. They are also good at following directions.

■ Achievement Profile Keys

- **Ability to save money.** Every company seeks to minimize its expenses.

Employers' Most Wanted List

Employers are searching for candidates with a few highly desirable traits. Among them:

1.	Attention to detail	98%
2.	Reading skills	95%
3.	Ability to cooperate with people	94%
4.	Willingness to make an extra effort to increase quality of performance	92%
5.	Ability to work under pressure	91%
6.	Verbal and communication skills	90%
7.	Ability to manage time, be productive	89%
8.	Ability to adapt, be flexible	89%
9.	Ability to solve problems	84%
10.	Ability to interpret and integrate information	83%
11.	Ability to set priorities	82%
12.	Good grooming and personal hygiene	79%
13.	Writing skills	79%
14.	Math skills	74%

Source: *Career Source*, 1997–98 edition

- **Ability to save time.** Your productivity ultimately saves the company money. Someone who can follow procedures or recommend improvements to existing procedures will enhance the company's organization and, ultimately, profitability.

- **Ability to earn money.** If you can contribute to the bottom line, you are an asset to any company.

EXERCISE

Go through the list of profile keys and check which ones you think apply to you. Then select one trait from each of the keys—Personal, Professional, and Achievement—and briefly write about a situation in which you applied that trait, whether at school, home, or a job. You should end up with a total of three different stories.

Example: From the list of Professional Profile Keys, dedication: Once when a co-worker called in sick, you worked a double shift to complete an important project within the deadline.

Once you have identified specific situations in which you applied these positive traits, you'll be prepared to share these anecdotes with an interviewer should the appropriate opportunity present itself.

Mind Your Body Language

When you interview for a job, it's important to make the best impression you can. To do so, you should monitor not only *what* you say but *how* you say it. Did you know that people show 55 percent of their feelings and emotions nonverbally? Thirty-eight percent of a message is carried by tone of voice. Only 7 percent of your feelings and emotions are conveyed by the actual words you use.

Your "silent" message is conveyed through signals in your body language. Positive signals can indicate agreement, openness, acceptance, and interest. Negative signals can reveal disagreement, suspicion, rejection, and defensiveness. Become attuned to the nonverbal signals you're giving and watch others to determine their receptiveness to you.

Positive Signals	Negative Signals
Good eye contact	Poor eye contact
Leaning forward	Slumping or turning away
Uncrossing arms or legs	Crossing arms or legs
Nodding head in approval	Shaking head in disapproval
Smiling, occasional laughing	No response
Unbuttoning jacket	Buttoning jacket
Rapt attention	Doodling or blank stare
Palms or wrists turned outward, open	Hands in pockets
Raised eyebrows	Narrowed eyes, sideways glances
Steepling fingers	Making a fist

As you observe and interpret body language, remember that each separate signal may not be a definitive indicator of a person's emotions. Different people have their own mannerisms or habits, so it is best to evaluate clusters or groups of signals to decipher the true message.

In an interview, it may be particularly helpful to monitor not only your own, but also the interviewer's, body language for instant feedback on how you're doing. If you receive positive signals while discussing a certain area, continue talking in the same vein. If you detect negative signals, try to modify your approach.

When meeting a prospective employer for an interview, be sure to make good eye contact and give a firm, confident handshake. (© Frank Siteman/Stock Boston)

You may find, too, that the interviewer begins to imitate your signals. For example, when you lean forward, the interviewer may do the same. This copying of signals usually indicates agreement, and you may even encourage a good reaction from the interviewer by subtly copying his or her signals.

After the Interview: Follow Up

EXERCISE

EXERCISE

Interview Self-Evaluation

The interview is over. Now is the time to assess yourself so that every interview, good or bad, can be a learning experience.

Complete the following statements about your last interview. Photocopy this Interview Self-Evaluation for future use.

1. I would describe my initial greeting with the interviewer as _____
_____ .

2. I was good at _____ .

3. I would improve _____ .

4. My appearance was _____ .

5. The next time I dress for an interview, I'll _____
_____ .

6. I was   ❑   on time   ❑   late   ❑   early.

7. When I spoke during the interview, my voice was _____
_____ .

8. My body language and eye contact during the interview could be described as _____
_____ .

9. The interviewer was more interested in   ❑   talking   ❑   listening. I adjusted my interview style accordingly by _____ .

10. I conveyed the following points about my skills: _____
_____ .

11. The toughest question I faced was _____ .
I handled this question _____ . The next time I'm asked about that I'll _____
_____ .

12. My overall mood and degree of relaxation was _____
_____ .

13. My strengths during today's interview were _____
_____ .

14. I'd like to improve the following for next time: _____
_____ .

15. Here is a list of things I need to do next to land this job:

    a. Thank-you letters _____

    b. Follow-up phone calls _____

    c. Other _____
    _____
    _____

14 Hill Street
Middletown, KY 83012
March 3, 2000

Mr. Michael Quinn, President
Technopro, Inc.
672 Charles Avenue
Bedford, KY 83102

Dear Mr. Quinn:

Thank you for taking the time to meet with me on Monday. I enjoyed touring Technopro and learning more about your business.

As I mentioned in the interview, I would be very interested in the bookkeeper position and feel I could be an asset to Technopro. Thank you for your consideration. I look forward to hearing from you soon.

Sincerely,

Lindsay Dorsett

Lindsay Dorsett

Sample Thank-You Letter to Follow Up Immediately After Interview (may be typed or handwritten)

CAREER-SEARCH ORGANIZATION CHART

Remember, looking for a job is your full-time job. Use the chart below to organize your search. Add dates to the chart as you complete each step. Before beginning, photocopy this chart for future use.

Prospective Employer Contact Person, Title Address/Phone	Research Completed	Date Inquiry Letter Sent	Date Cover Letter/ Résumé Sent	Date Follow-Up Phone Call	Interview Date/Time	Thank-You Note Sent	Remarks

Nontraditional Ways to Get an Interview

Occasionally, the job hunter needs to try something unique to get a foot in the door. Although networking, telephone calls, and letters are the traditional approaches to securing an interview, you may reach the point where you're ready to become more creative and more aggressive.

A WARNING: Not all employers endorse these approaches. Consider how conservative your career field is, what traditional methods you haven't yet tried, and what you have to lose. Remember, too, that some career experts swear that unorthodox approaches are the best. Use your best judgment, and when you've carefully considered your options, make a plan.

1. Send your résumé to the person you'd like to work for via an express mail service or courier marked "Personal and Confidential."

2. Get creative with your résumé. Make it very large or very small, make a puzzle out of it, or print it on neon orange paper. In your cover letter, explain your unusual presentation. For example, you might start out, "I'm the piece of the puzzle Brown, Incorporated, has been looking for." Accompany a tiny résumé with a letter that begins, "Sometimes it's easy to overlook the obvious choice."

3. Send a videotaped résumé.

4. Create a business card giving your name, phone number, and a few of your best qualifications. When you meet potential contacts, give them your card.

5. Put a position wanted ad in the newspaper.

6. Learn whether the prospective employer belongs to any local clubs or organizations. Go to a meeting to network and introduce yourself.

7. Send a clever e-mail to your prospect.

8. Send a series of postcards. The first might read, "Wish I was there." Send more information on each one.

9. Learn what the employer's hobby is. Send an appropriate item. For example, you might send an avid sailor a model sailboat. You may need to enlist the aid of a secretary to find out this information. These small gifts might also be more appropriate after the interview.

10. Send an object related to your name. Reginald King might send a crown; Dawn Greenleaf might send a pressed four-leaf clover.

11. Send a photograph with your résumé printed on the reverse.

12. Send an unusual object with an explanation. For example, send some shoelaces with a note that reads, "I'm sorry you've been tied up, but I'm hoping we can get off on the right foot?" Send a jar of cinnamon with a few words about how you can add spice to the company.

EXERCISE

Brainstorm two or three other methods that might be suitable for your career field or position. Write them here.

1. _____

2. _____

3. _____

4. _____

5. _____

When you've committed yourself to one of these guerrilla tactics, carry it off with confidence and enthusiasm. It may turn out to be the most profitable and memorable of your job-hunting experiences.

Reasons for Unsuccessful Interviews

Job applicants are frequently rejected because of the following behaviors or characteristics:

1. Too interested in starting salary
2. Uncertainty on wants in job/career or long-range goals
3. Poor personal appearance
4. Overbearing, overaggressive, conceited, "know-it-all"
5. Inability to express self clearly—poor voice, diction, grammar
6. Lack of interest and enthusiasm—passive, indifferent
7. Lack of confidence and poise—nervous, ill at ease
8. Poor scholastic record—just got by
9. Unwilling to start at the bottom—expects too much too soon
10. Makes excuses—evasive, hedges on unfavorable factors in record
11. Lack of tact

12. Condemnation of past employers

13. Lack of maturity

14. Lack of courtesy—ill-mannered

15. Marked dislike for schoolwork

16. Lack of vitality

17. Fails to look interviewer in the eye

18. Limp, fishlike handshake

19. Loafs during vacations

20. Unhappy married life

21. Friction with parents

22. Sloppy application blank

23. Merely shopping around

24. Wants job only for a short time

25. Little sense of humor

26. No interest in company or in industry

27. Lack of knowledge in field of specialization

28. Parents make all major decisions

29. Emphasis on whom he knows

30. Cynical

31. Lazy

32. Intolerant—strong prejudices

33. Narrow interests

34. Inability to take criticism

35. Lack of appreciation of the value of experience

36. Radical ideas

37. Late to interview without good reason

38. Knows nothing about company

39. Fails to express appreciation for interviewer's time

40. Asks no questions about the job

EXERCISE

See if you can come up with a few reasons of your own why someone might "fail" an interview.

1. _____

2. _____

3. _____

Select three inappropriate interview characteristics from the above list or from your own responses, and brainstorm ways to remedy these negatives. For example, if you select item no. 16, lack of vitality, you could develop ways to specifically convey your energy and vitality to an interviewer, such as by extending a firm handshake and an enthusiastic greeting.

Handling Rejection

KEY POINT

Nobody likes to be rejected, but everybody goes through it at some time in his or her career. Remember that fact as you seek employment. Many people spend months searching and interview for dozens of jobs before they receive an appealing offer. When the economy is depressed, months can even turn into years until the right position turns up. So don't get discouraged if you don't achieve instant success.

When you're first making the rounds, try not to be personally offended if potential employers don't return your calls. Realize that they may be busy doing their work and that your call represents an interruption in their day, certainly not a priority.

Likewise, try not to take it personally if you are not offered a job after having what you consider a successful interview. You may feel that you are perfectly suited to handle a particular position, but the employer may not. There may be other candidates who have more experience, skills that more precisely match the job's responsibilities, lower salary requirements, or a personality more compatible with management practices. Often, you may be rejected for reasons that have absolutely nothing to do with you.

Look upon every rejection as a learning experience. Try to determine why the outcome was not what you wanted. Look for specific ways to improve your presentation. Remember that finding a job is a numbers game: The more people you contact and the more interviews you have, the more likely you are to land a job.

■ The Right Frame of Mind

Rare is the individual who begins job hunting and is immediately offered the quintessential dream job. Most job hunts take time and effort. You'll be better equipped to handle a challenging job search if you maintain a positive attitude. Keep these tips in mind:

1. **Believe in yourself.** You've worked hard to get where you are today. You've acquired the skills you need. Now it's just a matter of time until you find an opportunity to put them to use. Dare to dream. Pursue ideas and opportunities that are of interest and value to you. Exude confidence in all you do.

2. **Look at the big picture.** Don't let the little things get you down. Learn from your mistakes. Keep your perspective and focus on what's important.

3. **Don't feel angry or bitter.** It's easy to be mad at employers who don't recognize the wonderful asset you could be to their companies, but don't internalize the rejection. Besides being self-destructive, your anger will come through in future interviews.

4. **Be creative.** Don't give up. Find unique solutions to problems. Keep generating new ideas. Think beyond the traditional answers. Look for a market niche, and develop a creative way to fill that niche.

5. **Be flexible.** Plan your job search, but reevaluate and change your plan as you learn new things and meet new people. Expect the unexpected. Develop contingency plans to handle different situations.

6. **Be optimistic.** Focus on the positive aspects of even negative occurrences. If one approach fails, be prepared to try another.

7. **Don't be afraid to take risks.** Accept the fact that finding, and eventually accepting, a new job involves an element of risk. Learn to manage the risks by identifying them and then limiting their downside.

8. **Be persistent.** Keep your attention focused on the task at hand. Don't give up until you've found an avenue to success. Keep exploring solutions until you find one that works.

9. **Take an action orientation.** Be a doer. Be a decision maker. Take control of a situation and propel yourself toward success.

10. **Have a "Plan B."** If your career path is not a smooth one, perhaps it's time to reassess your strategy and goals.

Ask for What You Want

Some job hunters make the mistake of forgetting to ask for what they want. Either because they are too timid or because they assume the employer knows their intentions, many people find themselves unpleasantly surprised and disappointed during different phases of their job hunt.

DIVE IN   At each step of the search, keep your goal in mind and be sure to clearly communicate it to the appropriate people.

- When researching, don't just wander around the library waiting for the appropriate field to present itself. Work up a few topic areas from which to start. Ask the librarian for the kind of help you need, for example, where to find articles on manufacturing or where to find phone books for Denver.

- In your cover letter, remember to ask for the interview. Specify what you plan to do next: follow up with a phone call or a visit. Don't wait for the employer to call you. Follow up each letter promptly.

- In the interview, close by asking for the job (assuming that you still want it). Tell interviewers that it's been a pleasure meeting them and that you'd enjoy working with them. Make it clear to them that you want the position. Be enthusiastic and positive.

- In your thank-you notes and in all other follow-up letters, state that you are well suited to the responsibility and challenge of the position. At each phase of your job hunt, a small goal should be clear in your mind. Sometimes, stating these goals aloud or writing them down can help you achieve them.

■ A Final Note on Follow-up

KEY POINT

It bears repeating that a good indicator of a job hunter's follow-through, etiquette, and attention to detail is the thank-you note. This small gesture has a big impact and should be considered essential after the interview. Very few job hunters remember this important step. Those who do stand out. They are also able to put their names across the employer's desk one more time while creating good will and a lasting, positive impression.

Passing the Test

Employment Tests

Because hiring the right employees is so critical to a company's success, many employers require their candidates to take certain tests. Drug testing is becoming more popular each year. Proficiency or competency tests that measure an applicant's abilities in a specific area are also common. Medical exams check an applicant's overall health and physical ability to do a job. For professional positions, psychological tests have gained popularity in helping employers correctly match candidates with the responsibilities of a position.

Your prospective employer will tell you which tests are required and will give you instructions for taking them.

■ Drug Testing of Job Applicants

KEY POINT

Because of the problems a drug user can bring to the job, more and more employers are beginning to require preemployment blood or urine tests. These tests reveal the presence of cocaine, marijuana, opiates, amphetamines, and barbiturates.

Although some employers will provide assistance and counseling to workers who have been with the company for a while before they develop a drug problem, they are unlikely to take on a new worker who shows signs of drug abuse. Their reasoning is sound: Drug abuse is likely to cost the company in terms of increased absenteeism, increased chance of on-the-job mistakes or accidents, and potential for embarrassment should customers learn of the problem. In addition, alcohol and drug abuse may ultimately raise the company's insurance costs.

Current estimates reveal that nearly 50 percent of employers test college recruits for drug use. That figure is likely to rise in future years as more employers become aware of the difficulties associated with workers who have substance-abuse problems.

■ Skills Tests

Depending on the type of job you apply for, you may be asked to take tests that measure a specific ability. Some examples:

- A data entry clerk might take a typing test.
- A secretary might take typing, spelling, and computer skills tests.
- A telemarketer might take a speech/voice test.
- A bookkeeper might take a math skills test.
- A reporter might take a writing skills test.
- A dancer might have to audition.

Because hiring the right employee is so critical to a company's success, you may be asked to take a skills test that measures a specific ability required for the job you want. (© Bob Daemmrich/The Image Works)

You most likely can't cram for this type of exam, but you can put your mind at ease by knowing what to expect. Attempt to find out all you can about the test beforehand. Try to relax so that your true skills will be apparent. Also, as you're taking the test, remember that it is probably not the deciding factor in whether or not you are hired. It is just another element to help the employer get a true picture of your capabilities.

■ Psychological Tests

There is increasing recognition that interpersonal style is just as important as technical skills in being successful. Therefore, some professional jobs today require that you take a psychological test. Unlike most tests you've probably encountered in your schooling and in real life, this is not a pass-or-fail type of exam, and there are no right or wrong answers. It's a test to determine such things as your personality, your ability to get along with others, how you handle stress, whether you're honest, and the amount of energy you'll bring to the job. It may also be used to identify the kind of position in which you would be most successful.

In 1989, Congress banned most private-sector applications of the polygraph test, voice stress analysis, and other electronic screening methods. Many private employers who previously depended on these tests have turned to psychological testing to select the best job applicants.

Psychological tests usually consist of about fifty multiple-choice questions. Sometimes tests are "graded" in house; other times they are sent for evaluation to the firm that created the test. Results may be in the form of a description of the applicant's personality or may simply say whether the applicant is recommended for hire or should be considered with caution.

The key to success on a psychological test is to answer the questions as you view yourself for the professional position for which you are applying. Don't answer the questions as the kind of person you see yourself in your personal life unless it is identical to your professional persona. That is, don't lie or compromise your personal integrity, but be aware of the fact that as a student or working professional you've learned a set of behavioral patterns that enable you to be successful and productive. It is those behavioral patterns that determine whether you will make a good hire. Take the psychological test with these two strategies in mind:

1. As you answer each question, think to yourself: How has my experience as a student or a professional taught me to think and respond to this? Use your learned and developed professional behavior traits to select the correct answer.

2. Look at yourself from the employer's point of view. Evaluate which traits come into play that enable you to handle your responsibilities effectively. Those are the traits you want to call attention to in your psychological test.

Most likely, you will have no time limit imposed on taking the test. So make sure that you take the time to consider each question carefully. Be aware that the test may contain "double blinds," in which you are asked a question on page one and then asked almost the same question worded slightly differently about thirty or forty questions later. The technique is based on the belief that most of us can tell a lie but few of us can remember that lie under stress, and will therefore answer the question differently later.

You are likely to encounter ethics questions, such as, "Have you ever stolen anything?" or "Have you ever told a lie?" The goal of the employer is to determine if you will be an honest employee.

KEY POINT

Don't seek to project a false image of yourself by the answers you select. Employers are simply looking for people who will fit into their corporate culture and who have well-adjusted personal and professional lives.

Unfortunately, you will probably never find out exactly how you did on the test or what it revealed about your personality. Employers are careful to avoid saying anything that could expose them to a discrimination lawsuit. If you get the job, you'll know you did fine. If not, don't assume you "failed" the psychological test. As you know by now, job applicants are selected or not selected for a myriad of reasons. Learn from the experience, and move on to your next job-hunting adventure.

■ Physicals

You may be asked to have a medical exam as a condition of employment. In some cases, you'll be able to see your own doctor. In others, you might be asked to see a physician who has been contracted by the employer.

A medical exam is allowable only after an offer is extended and only if it is job related and required of all new employees in the same job category. The job offer may be contingent on the successful outcome of the exam.

Physical agility tests are not considered medical exams and may be given at any point in the application or employment process. Tests must be job related and administered to all applicants or employees in a job category.

The reason for medical exams and physical agility tests is twofold: to evaluate your physical health before the job begins and to ensure that your physical capabilities, with or without accommodation, will meet the demands of the job.

■ Probation Period

Over the years, the costs of hiring and training new employees have skyrocketed, causing some employers to insist on a probation period for new hires. This period, usually lasting from one to three months, gives the employer an opportunity to evaluate your skills and see if your personality is a match for the company. During the trial period, you will most likely not be given any benefits or health insurance coverage, once again saving money and protecting the employer in case you don't work out.

If an employer says you must go through a probation period, don't take it personally. It is probably standard operating procedure for that type of position. However, you should be clear in finding out what the terms of your employment will be after probation. Clarify items such as the following:

- Salary

- Health insurance

- Other benefits

- Vacation time, i.e., does your probation period count toward earned vacation time?

- Salary review—if the terms of your hiring state you will be reviewed in one year, clarify whether that year will include the time served while on probation.

CHAPTER 12

Backdoor Your Way into a Job

Taking an Indirect Approach to Job Hunting

It is sometimes difficult for first-time job hunters to obtain a position in their field or even to decide what position they want. If you fall into this category, you may want to consider a less direct approach to job hunting, such as a part-time job, temporary help, freelancing, an entry-level position, internship, or volunteer work.

■ Multiple Jobs for Experience and Contacts

It would be great if, before you graduated, you had employers begging you to come to work. You could name your salary and your terms. And you'd be doing the job you always dreamed of. Unfortunately, for most of us, that's not the case. If finding that dream job isn't as easy as you thought, you might consider another tactic—getting multiple jobs. Sounds crazy, doesn't it? You can't find one good job, so try to find two. The fact is, you may be able to land a part-time position, a volunteer job, an internship, or a freelance situation to help get your feet wet in your field.

Second jobs—or even third or fourth ones—are becoming common in today's labor market. They're a means to supplement incomes, explore a career, establish a backup job for security, or prepare to segue to something more fulfilling.

The best type of second job is one that is related to your field. Even if it isn't the type of position you'd want on a permanent basis, it can flesh out your résumé and help you gain contacts.

For example, if you're hoping to become a teacher but full-time teaching positions are few and far between, consider signing on as a substitute. Chances are, the income from substitute teaching won't be enough for you to live on, but when combined with another job, it could help you to get by. Best of all, you'll be gaining experience in your field and making contacts. When a full-time teaching position becomes available, you'll be an obvious contender.

As an aspiring teacher, you can even consider private tutoring. Or think about teaching an aerobics class or working part-time in a day care center, after-school program, or recreational center.

If you'd like to be a reporter or photographer for a daily newspaper but are having trouble finding that first job, approach a small weekly or monthly publication as a freelancer. Once again, the income will be small, but the rewards in terms of potential opportunity and experience will be great.

If you're hoping to become a veterinarian, apply at the local animal shelter. If you'd like to be a corporate manager one day, start your own small business on the side. Maybe you do landscaping, word processing, disk jockeying at parties, or sales for companies such as Tupperware Company International or Mary Kay Cosmetics. The skills you develop in scheduling, organization, and money management can be transferred to any job.

Having two jobs simultaneously isn't for everyone. It requires abundant energy, extraordinary time-management skills, and lots of "self" skills: self-discipline, self-sacrifice, self-marketing, and enough self-awareness to know your limits. To succeed, try not to think of it as just another job. Don't compete with or compromise any of your employers. And don't try to do too much.

EXERCISE

Take a moment to consider whether a second job makes sense for you. Complete the following:

List your career choice(s): _____

Brainstorm some practical ideas for part-time, supplemental, or volunteer jobs that could eventually help you to land your dream position.

1. _____

2. _____

3. _____

List some specific ways that you can go about finding that supplemental job.

1. _____

2. _____

3. _____

Interview someone with multiple jobs and ask them to discuss the positives and negatives of their experience.

■ Temping

One of the best ways to obtain a full-time job is to start off as a temporary employee. It gets your foot in the door and allows you an opportunity to prove yourself. More importantly, it's an ideal way for you to evaluate a company and decide if it's one you'd like to work for permanently.

Getting a temporary job tends to be much easier than finding permanent work. The easiest way to find temporary work is to register with a temporary service, or maybe with several services. Having your name on file with more than one agency helps ensure that you'll be kept working with less downtime and that you'll have more potential assignments from which to choose.

To find the right temporary agencies, you can ask friends and networking contacts for their suggestions. You can also check your local Yellow Pages. Or you can call companies that you'd like to work for and ask their human resources department which temporary services they use. If you're fortunate enough to be in a field such as computers, accounting, health care, or sales, you may find a temporary agency that specializes in that area.

Next, contact the service and briefly describe your skills. Most services will invite you in for an interview. Your interview will consist of filling out a lengthy application form and meeting with a representative. Be sure to bring along a current copy of your résumé. If you're seeking a position in an office environment, most likely you'll be asked to take a battery of tests on the computer. Your typing skills and knowledge of various software programs will be evaluated.

Be sure to tell the representative the kinds of positions you'll consider. The better temporary services go out of their way to offer you assignments that meet your criteria, but you have to communicate those criteria early in the game. Unfortunately, most temporary agencies specialize in clerical or industrial jobs. Even though you may aspire to be a manager at a business, you're more likely to be placed in a secretarial job. Don't be discouraged. Remember that this is a temporary position.

At the interview, don't be shy about asking questions. Find out how the temporary service operates. Determine how the representative intends to match you with an employer. Don't be embarrassed to talk about money. Most likely, you'll be paid an hourly fee that will vary from one assignment to the next. Be clear to your representative about the pay scale you'll consider. If you have good skills, you'll be selected for higher-paying jobs.

Depending on the local area you're in, the specific temporary service, and the diversity of your skills, you could be offered a job immediately or not for months. Don't hesitate to call your temporary service on a regular basis to check on job availability. Often, it's the most motivated workers whom the representatives place first.

Once you're given an assignment, try to get as much information as possible from the temporary service. Besides the basics of when and where to report, get a feel for the type of work you'll be expected to do.

At the job, adopt a full-time mindset. Approach the position as though you'll be working there permanently and you'll make a good impression. A good attitude is vital.

Don't expect to be treated like a savior. Most likely, you're simply filling in for someone who's sick, on vacation, overworked, or being replaced. Don't force yourself on others. Remember, you're not one of the gang, so don't take it personally if full-timers don't go out of their way to make you feel at home.

While you're working, keep your eyes open for opportunities. Many temporary employees get offered full-time work if they prove themselves capable and likable. If a position is not available, your immediate supervisors can pass your name along to departments that are hiring or even give you the names of their own personal contacts outside the company.

While temping, don't give up your search for a permanent position. Try to use your lunch hour to make phone calls. Schedule interview appointments for after hours or early morning.

Temporary work gives you income and puts you in the work force in the path of potential job opportunities. It's a great way to learn about different companies and industries. You'll have a chance to polish your skills and meet new people. View temping as a part of your education and the job-hunting process, and the experience will be worthwhile.

Use the Internet for further information about temping and networking. Net-Temps at www.net_temps.com/ is a giant site that lists many good, quality temporary jobs.

■ Freelancing

Many a full-time employee started out as a freelancer or contractor. What exactly is a freelancer? Someone who is self-employed selling his or her unique services to multiple companies.

The word *freelance* comes from the Middle Ages, when a knight would offer his lance and, with it, his allegiance to the lord with the most money. Today's freelancers offer their special skills to companies who pay for their services.

Companies hire freelancers when they need an individual with a specific talent, have a temporary work overload, or simply don't want to incur the expenses and responsibilities of a full-time employee.

Typically, freelancing is associated with such fields as publishing and the arts. However, in today's ever-dynamic marketplace, freelance opportunities exist in many fields. Architects, writers, artists, secretaries, photographers, computer programmers, software engineers, nurses, and television producers are just a few of the many professionals who freelance.

To be successful as a freelancer, you'll need a marketable skill and the persistence to develop a stable of clients. Sales is a major component of successful freelancing. As a freelancer, you essentially run your own business, making you solely responsible for the bottom line. On the plus side, you'll have independence, scheduling flexibility, and the financial rewards of being your own boss.

Freelancing can be a full-time undertaking or a means to an end. It is a great way to backdoor your way to a full-time job. As a freelancer, you have an opportunity to prove to an employer what a valuable asset you can be. And you'll have a chance to get to know the people who can recommend or hire you when a full-time position at the firm becomes available.

■ Entry-Level Positions

Secretarial or mailroom work may not be your idea of the perfect job; however, it may be a way to land that first career position. Entry-level positions won't provide the salary or prestige you had hoped for, but they can get you in the door for a position in your field. There are many success stories of famous businesspeople and celebrities who started at the bottom.

If you've studied advertising, you might seek a job as an administrative assistant or account coordinator in an ad agency. You'll get to know the firm's clients, its methods of doing business, and the specific types of accounts it handles. Most importantly, you'll learn how an ad agency functions. If you've studied television production and aspire to be a director one day, you may be able to get a job as a gofer, doing whatever extra tasks need to be done, from photocopying scripts to taking phone messages. If you've studied physical therapy, you may be able to get a job setting appointments or greeting patients.

By now, you've realized that you're not going to start out as a president or chief executive officer of a firm. The first stage of your career development will most likely involve "paying your dues." An entry-level position for which you may be somewhat overqualified and underpaid could be a springboard to great things. Swallow your pride, work hard, and keep your eyes open for the next great opportunity.

■ Internships

Whether you are still in school or have already graduated, you may be able to obtain an internship in your field of study. Most internships are unpaid or include only a small stipend. Some count as credit toward your degree. Although working for free may not seem appealing at first, consider this: Many top executives got their start through an internship program.

As an intern, you may be saddled with some of the less glamorous tasks of the job you aspire to have one day, but you'll be getting firsthand, on-the-job experience. You'll be making contacts and developing the skills you need to succeed in your chosen career.

Many interns are hired once a position opens up—there's something to be said for being in the right place at the right time. If an internship is financially impractical for you, consider arranging a part-time internship that would allow you to keep a paying job at the same time.

Finding an internship.   Your best chance of learning about internship opportunities is through college placement offices. They frequently receive notices of internships from both local and national companies. In fact, many companies even do their interviewing right on campus, using the placement office to prequalify applicants. Some college placement offices don't even require that you be a student of their school to participate.

INTERNET

Check out sources on the Internet as well. Just as many companies list job openings at their web site, they also list internship opportunities. Some of the major career sites also include internships. At JobTrak at www.jobtrak.com, you'll find thousands of internships listed. However, it can be searched only if your school participates in the service. Check with your campus placement office to obtain a password, which you'll need to access the site's data bank. For internship listings, you can also try Rising Start Internships, at www.rsinternships.com and 4Work.com, at www.4work.com.

Use networking to find out about internships. Many internships are not publicized. They are filled with people who learned of the internships via contacts.

There are many good directories on the market that list thousands of internship opportunities across the country and even abroad. These books usually categorize internships by career field, location, and organization name. You may also find details about duties, compensation, and competitiveness.

If a company that you would like to work for has no current job openings, ask if it has an internship program. If so, you may be able to use an internship as a steppingstone to a real job. If not, consider sending a letter that proposes an internship, clearly explaining how the company can benefit from bringing you on in that capacity.

What to look for in an internship. A good internship is one that includes more than "busy work." If the only thing that you learn while interning is how to make good coffee, your experience will have been a waste of time. Seek an internship that can afford some opportunity to work on stimulating projects.

If your college internship coordinator does not already do so, develop a "learning contract" in which you state your learning objectives and spell out specific tasks and responsibilities. Put the contract in writing and have your supervisor sign it. At various points in your internship, refer to the contract to be sure you are meeting its criteria.

At your internship, try to find good role models. You can learn specific career skills from someone who is seasoned and successful. If possible, cultivate a mentor relationship with someone who can take you under his or her wing.

Finally, seek opportunities during your internship to broaden your knowledge of the field by attending conferences, seminars, and trade shows.

■ Volunteer Work

Although all students dream of earning "big bucks" when they graduate, depending on your career choice and the state of the economy, that may not be possible. In the first few years of your career, your focus should be on gaining valuable work experience, not the size of your salary.

One of the ways to gain entry into your career field may be through volunteer work. Offering your time to a company or organization can get you in the door as well as allow you to explore possible career options. As a volunteer, you'll probably be able to set your own hours, allowing you to hold a paying job as well.

Nonprofit or service organizations are usually the most receptive to working with volunteers. Some examples of organizations that often depend on volunteers are the United Way, the American Red Cross, libraries, and hospitals. Of course, every community differs, so you'll have to do your own research to find out about the best opportunities. Whether you are seeking a career in computers, public relations, office management, accounting, or health services, there should be some kind of volunteer position that would provide you with worthwhile experience and the chance to make contacts.

A good source for learning about organizations that welcome volunteers is the annual *Volunteer Center Member Directory*, published by the Points of Light Foundation. It lists Volunteer Centers and other volunteer-referring agencies for each state. Volunteer Centers collect information from organizations about what kinds of volunteers they need. You may be able to find a copy at the library or order your own by writing the Points of Light Foundation, 1737 H Street, N.W., Washington, DC 20006, or by calling (202) 223-9186 or toll free (800) 272-8306.

Make volunteering a worthwhile experience.   Even though you don't receive a salary for your work, don't take your responsibilities lightly. To make the most of the situation, volunteer for an organization that you are interested in or that has relevance to your career. Work as closely as you can with professionals who can serve as role models to you. Seek out training within the organization. Every skill you master makes you a smarter, more employable person. Ask to be "promoted" to tasks of greater challenge so that your volunteer experience is filled with accomplishments.

Be sure to list your volunteer work on your résumé along with your paid jobs. Your achievements as a volunteer are significant. Potential employers will appreciate your initiative.

CHAPTER 13

Organizing and Surviving the Job Hunt

Take Care of Yourself

Aside from searching for a job that's right for you, there's something else you should take care of—yourself! A job search takes time. People seeking entry-level or generalized positions can expect their search to take two to four months; those seeking higher-paying or more-specialized jobs can expect a search period to last six months, a year, or more. Also, the state of the employment situation in your field and locale will affect the length of your search.

How does one survive such a long and potentially stressful period of time? Concentrate on the following four pieces of advice.

■ 1. Think of Job Hunting as Your Job

Don't consider this time to be a vacation, and don't let anyone else think of your job search that way either. Get up early, get dressed, and go to a spot where you can plan your day. Stake out an area to use as your office, and have all your job-search materials ready. Even if you can't convert a spare bedroom or alcove into an office, assemble in one spot your résumés, stationery, computer, stamps, lists and organizational charts, and, most importantly, a phone. An answering machine might also prove to be a worthwhile investment.

Whatever you do, don't sleep until noon and lounge around in a sweatsuit with a bowl of munchies. This mentality and behavior is counterproductive. If you need to take a long weekend for a vacation, do it. Then resume your search. Be wary of those who ask you to run errands, baby-sit, or do other chores "because you have all that free time." Establish in your own mind and in the minds of others that, for now at least, finding the right job is your primary occupation.

■ 2. Practice Time Management and Self-Discipline

Make a "do list" each day and prioritize each item with an A (most important), B (important), or C (least important). Group errands when possible. For example, when you're downtown doing research at the library, you may also plan to drop by the post office to buy stamps or mail letters. Build rewards into your day, too. Perhaps after you've accomplished all your morning tasks, you'll treat yourself and meet a friend for lunch.

Take pleasure in checking items off your list, and consider keeping all your lists together in one notebook or folder. Sometimes reviewing old lists can remind you of your accomplishments or give you new energy and direction. At the end or beginning of each day, evaluate the items left undone. Either replace the items on a new list or reassess and abandon them altogether. Careful time-management habits are essential to most occupations, and developing them now can be a skill you could mention in forthcoming interviews.

Examine the sample list that follows to see how one job hunter has organized and prioritized tasks:

SAMPLE JOB HUNTER'S DO LIST

Date: 10/27/00

Check When Completed	Priority	Task
❑	B	Dig up more leads using newspapers at the library.
❑	A	Make follow-up phone call to J. Curaci at XYZ Corp.
❑	A	Revise résumé objective to fit ad in the *Daily News.*
❑	A	Write thank-you letter to Mr. Lee at Lee's Widgets.
❑	B	Write cover letter for lead given by Uncle Joe.
❑	A	Write thank-you letter to Uncle Joe.
❑	C	Buy more matching envelopes at office supplies store.
❑	B	Call Barton's to find name of contact person.
❑	C	Stop by chamber of commerce for brochures or leads about local industry.

You could also take the next step and plan the order of your day, as shown here:

TIME PLANNER

A.M.	Goals
9:00–10:00	Make phone calls for leads, follow-up, etc.
10:00–11:30	Write letters; revise résumé.
11:30–12:00	Read annual reports and brochures picked up yesterday.

P.M.	
12:00–1:00	Meet Jane for lunch.
1:00–3:30	Research at library.
3:30–4:30	Stop by post office, chamber of commerce, office supplies store.
5:00–6:00	Attend Business After Hours meeting.

Forms to assist you in managing your time are provided on pages 170 and 171.

■ 3. Set Goals

Keep your purpose in mind and work toward it to stay productive. Write down your goals and review them periodically. Perhaps your daily goal might be to make two new contacts. A weekly goal might be to mail out twenty résumés and cover letters. Whatever you choose, make your goal specific and measurable, and set a deadline.

■ 4. Find Outlets for Stress

Do everything you can to keep yourself healthy and calm. Exercise is a great way to clear your head and relieve tension. Many people find relaxation techniques to be helpful. Build a support network of helpful friends and family. If the pressure becomes too intense, see a counselor or visit your rabbi or pastor. If possible, avoid people who discourage you or distract you from the goals you've set. Taking care of your mental and physical health will give you an edge in the job search.

(Photocopy for future use.)

JOB HUNTER'S DO LIST

Date: _____

Check When Completed	Priority (A/B/C)	Tasks

❏   _____   **1.** _____

❏   _____   **2.** _____

❏   _____   **3.** _____

❏   _____   **4.** _____

❏   _____   **5.** _____

❏   _____   **6.** _____

❏   _____   **7.** _____

❏   _____   **8.** _____

❏   _____   **9.** _____

❏   _____   **10.** _____

Goals

By today's end: _____

_____

By one week from today: _____

_____

Within one month: _____

_____

Within six months: _____

_____

Within one year: _____

_____

(Photocopy for future use.)

JOB HUNTER'S TIME PLANNER

Date: _____

A.M.	Tasks
8:00	
8:30	
9:00	
9:30	
10:00	
10:30	
11:00	
11:30	

P.M.	
12:00	
12:30	
1:00	
1:30	
2:00	
2:30	
3:00	
3:30	
4:00	
4:30	
5:00	
5:30	
6:00	
6:30	

Troubleshooting for Job Hunters

If after implementing all the job-hunting techniques mentioned in this guidebook you find you're still struggling with one or two particular areas, try some of these tips to help you over the trouble spots:

Having Trouble . . . ?	Try to . . .
• Identifying the type of job desired	Interview or job-shadow professionals in various fields.
	Peruse the Sunday classified ads in a major newspaper.
	Do further reading on jobs. Especially helpful is *The Occupational Outlook Handbook,* a government publication available in most libraries.
	Visit career web sites on the Internet.
• Identifying strengths	Brainstorm a list.
	Examine, in writing, areas of your past success.
	Ask a friend, family member, or teacher.
• Preparing a résumé	Work on only one section at a time.
	Show drafts to people whose opinion you trust.
	Experiment with new formats.
	Use the Internet to find posted résumés of others in your field.
• Generating leads	Read local newspapers and note active companies.
	Find new ways to network.
	Use the Internet to identify potential employers.
• Researching employers	Check the library.
	Visit chambers of commerce.
	Use the Internet.
• Using the Internet	Enlist the help of an Internet-savvy friend or teacher.
	Begin by visiting some of the general career web sites.

• Getting past the personnel office	Call or visit your potential supervisor directly, especially early or late in the day, after his or her assistant has left.
	Send an e-mail directly to the individual making the hiring decision.
• Networking	Persistence is the key. Join organizations in your field.
	Use networking groups.
	Talk to everyone about your situation.
	Join an on-line discussion group related to your career field.
• Writing cover letters	Read your drafts from last sentence to first to make sure each sentence alone makes sense.
	Review in writing your strengths as well as your goals.
	Allow drafts to sit for a day between revisions.
• Preparing for interviews	Practice in a mirror or with friends.
	Ask and answer questions using a tape recorder.
	Go to a job fair and get comfortable talking with recruiters.
• Keeping track of contacts and progress	Write notes on wall or desk calendars.
	Use "to do" lists; prioritize items on your list.
	Set aside a special time each day for record keeping.
	Organize your job search using a filing system.
• Overcoming shyness	Say an extra few words to everyone you meet, including cashiers, co-workers, and bank tellers.
	Consider the possibility that shyness means you're thinking only about yourself. Try to spend one day focusing on other people and their personalities.

Finally, remember that smart people realize when they need extra help. Most community mental health centers offer the services of professional career counselors, and fees are often based on a sliding scale. Colleges also have career counselors on staff, and the costs are included in your tuition. Career counselors can administer skills or personality inventories, provide you with contacts, review your résumé, or help you practice interviewing. Take advantage of all the help that is available to you!

Evaluating
Job Offers

Choose the Best Job for You

Congratulations! Your hard work and professionalism have won you several job offers. Now you have a decision that many people would love to face.

EXERCISE

Complete the following exercise step by step. The process may be time consuming, but good decisions require careful consideration.

Step 1

The chart below might help you evaluate your career options at this point. It lists a number of job variables; fill in the blank spaces at the bottom of the left-hand column with other factors that are important to you in weighing one position against another.

Rank	Job Variables	Job Option 1: Company Name	Job Option 2: Company Name	Job Option 3: Company Name
	Benefits			
	Service to others			
	Challenge			
	Creativity			
	Schedule			
	Status			
	Title			
	Responsibilities			
	Satisfaction			
	Salary			
	Acceptable commute			
	Good work environment			
	Appropriate training			
	Educational opportunities			
	Acceptable supervisor			

___ Possibility for promotion	___	___	___
___ Flexibility	___	___	___
___ ___	___	___	___
___ ___	___	___	___
___ ___	___	___	___
___ ___	___	___	___

Step 2

Now rank each job variable by its importance to you. Do some careful and honest self-evaluation to decide which aspects of employment you value most. Would you endure a long commute in order to earn a higher salary? Perhaps you need a company that provides in-house child care, or perhaps being able to work outdoors is extremely important to you. You might have added these factors to the bottom of the variable list. If you decide that a factor is unimportant to you, rank it last or cross it off the list.

Step 3

Circle your top five variables.

Step 4

Open your mind to any options you haven't yet given full consideration. Returning to school, traveling, joining the military, or returning to a former position might be considered at this point; don't rule out any feasible option yet. If you think of another option, write it under Job Option 3, or create a Job Option 4 in the margin.

Step 5

Finally, examine each job variable in light of each job option. Go to the blank under Job Option 1 and across from your number-one job variable. Mark the blank with a check, a check plus, or a check minus, indicating whether the job meets your needs, exceeds your expectations, or falls short of your requirements. Examine every job variable under Job Option 1 in this way. Do the same for Job Options 2 and 3. You may discover you aren't sure how a particular employment offer measures up to one of your requirements. Mark that blank with a question mark and be sure to include it on a list of questions to ask your contact person later (see below).

Step 6

Now you have carefully considered what is important to you in your career and you've also examined all your job options. Look carefully down the column under each option. Which column has the most check pluses in your top five priorities? This option is probably your best.

Job Option 1   **Questions to ask** _____ **(contact person)**

1. _____

2. _____

3. _____

Job Option 2   **Questions to ask** _____ **(contact person)**

1. _____

2. _____

3. _____

Job Option 3   **Questions to ask** _____ **(contact person)**

1. _____

2. _____

3. _____

Negotiate Your Salary

KEY POINT

Discuss salary with your prospective employer only after other items have been firmed up, since this is likely to be the biggest stumbling block. Also, you don't want to give the impression that the salary is the most important aspect of your employment. You want the employer to believe you are genuinely interested in the job and its responsibilities. However, don't ever accept a job without knowing the salary. Go into an interview prepared. Know how much you want to make and work toward that goal.

Before you discuss salary requirements with your potential employer:

1. Research the salary range for the position you're considering accepting. Try to find out what this type of position pays in your area. There are several ways to do this. Trade journals will often do salary surveys for their industry; check the library for the current year's issue. Call trade associations. Ask others in the field. Read classified ads, which often list salaries along with job requirements. Search the Internet.

INTERNET

Several Internet sites keep current salary data. Many major career sites list salaries. It is particularly useful if you're considering relocating, as it enables you to compare the salary for a specific position in your current location to the salary for that position where you want to move. At Salary Surveys at www.dbm.com/jobguide/salary.html, you'll find hundreds of salary listings for all different types of positions. Also, try the Bureau of Labor Statistics at stats.bls.gov/oco/oco1000.htm; Job Star, at jobstar.org/tools/salary/sal-surv.htm; WageWeb, at www.wageweb.com; and Career InfoNet, at www.ac-inet.org/occ-seal.htm.

2. Try to find out what the person who had the job before you was paid.

3. Decide how important salary is to you at this stage in your career. Will this job represent a good steppingstone or entrée into the company?

4. Remember that some jobs have flexible salaries and some do not. Try to determine into which category your position falls. Jobs requiring more advanced skills usually have more pay flexibility, since people's varied experience and credentials have to be taken into consideration.

5. Consider the health of the local economy. If the economy is weak, you'll have less negotiating power. If the economy is strong, you'll have more clout.

6. Assess the demand for your skills. If they are highly specialized, you may have an edge in negotiation. If they are more general and are shared with numerous other applicants for the job, you may not.

During salary negotiation:

1. Let the employer say the first number. Realize that this initial offer is most likely below what the company is actually willing to pay.

2. If you must state a figure, give a range you would consider. Try to watch your employer's body language and overall response to judge whether your range is in the ballpark. Remember, too, that many employers are good actors when it comes to negotiating salaries.

3. Be firm when stating your salary requirements, not wishy-washy. Say, "I want X" instead of "Well, I know this is probably too much, but I'd like to make X. Is that a problem?"

4. If the employer throws out a number, don't just accept it. Respond with "I was hoping for something closer to X." Make sure that "X" is an amount that is actually higher than you think you can get. This leaves room for compromise.

5. You can discuss your salary in weekly, monthly, or annual terms as long as you understand how the numbers add up or break down.

6. Should the employer ask what you made at your previous job, try to avoid the question, especially if you are seeking a large hike in pay. If push comes to shove, answer honestly, but explain that your responsibilities in this new position sound like they would be much more challenging.

7. Ask how often you might expect a salary review.

8. Find out how large raises are in terms of percentage of overall salary. Remember, the employer may exaggerate this claim.

9. Don't be lulled into accepting less now if the employer suggests you can renegotiate your salary in three to six months when you've proved yourself. By then, you'll have no leverage.

10. Think about whether you can afford to live on the salary being offered. Be sure to account for state and federal taxes, which will come out of your pay. Remember that the cost of living varies from place to place.

11. Take into consideration benefits such as health insurance, stock options, retirement investment programs, and vacation time.

12. Find out whether an amount is deducted from your salary for health insurance. Evaluate the quality of the health insurance plan. With medical costs skyrocketing, a good insurance plan can be an important benefit.

KEY POINT

13. When negotiating, focus on the qualities you bring to the job rather than the salary. The key is to make the employer feel you are worth the salary you want.

14. Get promises in writing. ("We'll review your salary in six months" and so on.)

15. Don't consider Christmas bonuses as part of your salary. You'll receive those bonuses only if the company is doing well and only at the discretion of the employer. Finally, you don't want to have to wait until Christmas to get your money.

16. If commissions are part of your salary, get some indication of realistic expectations. Remember that the employer will probably highlight the earnings of people who make the most in commissions while downplaying those of people who earn average or below-average commissions.

17. If you reach a critical impasse in the discussion, ask whether you can think about the salary and get back to the employer. This will provide an opportunity for tensions to subside and for you to assess your options.

The End Is in Sight

■ The Acceptance Letter

Once you've decided which job you want to take, it's time to wrap things up. The acceptance letter serves several purposes. It is an opportunity to thank the hiring party, to express enthusiasm for the position, and, most importantly, to define the terms of your employment as agreed upon in your negotiations. Send copies to every person who has been directly involved in the hiring process. (There may come a time down the road when you'll be glad you put this information in writing.) Your acceptance letter should include a statement of the following issues:

1. Your job title

2. Salary

3. Contract terms

4. Starting date

■ The Rejection Letter

You probably were beginning to think that employers are the only ones who get to write rejection letters. Not true. Here's your big chance. If you have decided against accepting a position you've been offered, you should take the time to formally decline in writing. You never know if one day you may be calling that employer back for a job, and you want to be remembered positively. Your letter to turn down a position should cover these issues:

1. A courteous thank you for the employer's time and consideration.

2. A brief explanation of why you are not accepting the position.

3. A statement of any hopes you may have to work with that employer in the future.

131 East Robin Street
Milville, Virginia 23331
July 12, 2000

Mr. John Michaels
Medco Ltd.
14 Collie Street
Kingston, Virginia 23332

Dear Mr. Michaels:

I was very pleased to receive your letter of July 5, 2000, offering me the job of secretary for Medco's southern division. The conditions of employment meet my requirements, and I would like to accept the position.

As per our agreement, I will begin work on July 30, 2000, at a starting salary of $25,000. I look forward to working with a company as dynamic and progressive as Medco.

Sincerely,

Mary Carlson

Mary Carlson

Letter to Accept a Position

10 Cypress Avenue
Hollywood, CA 91472
May 16, 2000

Ms. Sandra Miles
Marketing Director
Quistron Corp.
17 W. 4th Avenue
Hollywood, CA 91473

Dear Ms. Miles:

After much thought, I have decided not to accept the position in the Marketing Department of Quistron Corp. While I very much appreciate the offer, I feel the position is not in line with my goals at this stage in my career.

Thank you for taking the time to meet with me and consider my qualifications. Should my situation change, I will certainly contact you.

Cordially,

Janet Massi

Janet Massi

Letter to Reject a Position

Getting to Work

Your First Few Weeks on the Job

DIVE IN

Those first few weeks on the job are sure to be challenging. If you're like most people, you'll feel nervous and a bit unsure of yourself. Don't let your fears take over; it won't take long until you feel at home. Here are some things to keep in mind when you're starting out:

1. **Do your homework.** There's no reason for a new employee to walk in clueless. With the Internet and other sources of information, it's easy to research companies.

2. **Learn your company's policies and procedures.** Some companies have a formal orientation program for new employees, whereas others expect you to "learn as you work."

3. **Become aware of the corporate culture.** Be alert to how people communicate (meetings, memos, face to face, voice mail, or e-mail). Note how the company handles its communications with customers and vendors. Observe the unwritten dress code, and be sure your clothes are appropriate. Become aware of how many hours that people work. Some companies are strictly 9 to 5, whereas others expect their workers to put in longer days or take short lunch hours. (Be advised that most companies don't pay salaried workers for overtime.) Adapt your style to the company's.

4. **Don't try too hard.** Nobody expects you to accomplish miracles overnight. Give yourself time to learn the ropes or you will risk making serious gaffes. You may also offend people whose support you'll later need.

5. **Send thank-you messages to the people who helped you job hunt.** Write or type short notes to all the people you contacted when you were unemployed. Tell them about your new job, and thank them for their support. Your efforts will be appreciated and remembered.

6. **Be discreet about your salary.** It's unprofessional to discuss salary. Never ask or tell anyone about pay, for it will invariably come back to haunt you.

7. **Clarify expectations.** Determine the mission of the company and how your job fits into that mission. Identify immediate priorities that need to be addressed. Talk to your boss to learn what he or she expects from you.

8. **Identify the winners.** Figure out who the superstars are at your company. Usually, that's easy to do because they're well-known and respected. Observe the company's movers and shakers, and learn their secrets to success.

Your First Year on the Job

Your first year of employment will probably constitute the best of times as well as the worst. There's the excitement of being in a new position with new people

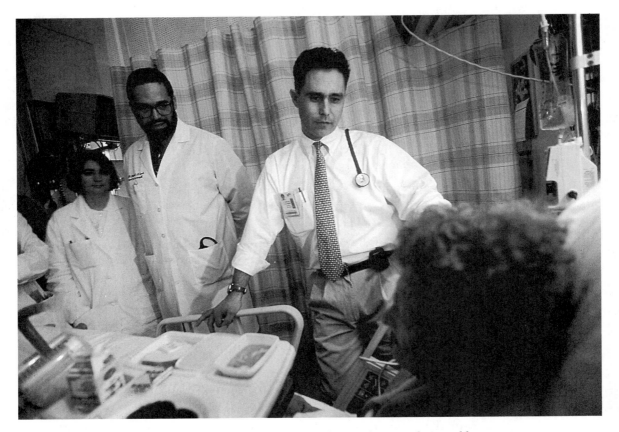

One of the most important tasks in your first year on the job is to observe others and learn as much as you can about your company and your individual responsibilities. (© Mark Richards/PhotoEdit)

and new responsibilities. But there are also the pressures of being the new kid on the block: your unfamiliarity with rules and policies, the difficulties of dealing with the different personalities of coworkers, and the politics of the corporate culture.

Most likely, your first year on the job will be a series of ups and downs, both successes and failures. However, there are some strategies you can employ to ensure that your initial year represents a solid beginning.

1. **Learn your job.** Become proficient at the responsibilities for which you were hired. Some people concentrate their efforts on getting promoted without focusing on the tasks at hand. For true on-the-job success, you need to learn to do a great job no matter how trivial your tasks might seem to you. Keep in mind that when you're starting out, part of your job is making your boss look good.

2. **Accept that you will make mistakes.** As you learn on the job, you will have your series of fumbles. Don't be too hard on yourself. What's more important is how you learn from those mistakes.

3. **Focus on performance and results.** Excuses, even the best ones, are not what bosses remember at review time. Solid, consistent performance is the only thing that really matters. Be conscientious and enthusiastic about your work.

4. **Meet deadlines.** In school, you were probably accustomed to having someone else set deadlines—dates that papers were due, final exams, final projects, and so forth. At work, you're often responsible for setting your own deadlines, or at least for recognizing when tasks need to be completed. Set parameters, and then be sure to meet them. Remember, performance is the only thing that counts.

5. **Persistence pays off.** In the beginning, a task may seem hard or overwhelming. Stay with it. Eventually you'll get the hang of it.

6. **Take initiative.** Don't be afraid to assume responsibility. Ask questions if you're unclear on something. Request assistance if you need it. Take on projects that others don't want. Show that you're a team player.

7. **Go the extra mile.** Always do more than what's expected of you, never less. Do it without being asked or expecting recognition for your efforts. Remember—attitude is everything.

8. **Use common sense.** Try to figure things out on your own before asking for help. Work on developing your own instincts. Be a good listener and you'll accelerate the learning process.

9. **Pay attention to detail.** Detail people get the job done right, leaving nothing to fall through the cracks.

10. **Make a good impression.** Everyone will be watching the new employee. The impressions you make during this first year will stick with you and set the course for your career.

11. **Dress appropriately.** Wear clothes and jewelry that demonstrate your professionalism. Practice good personal hygiene.

12. **Earn the respect of your coworkers and superiors.** This is the time to begin establishing your professional image. Let people know you're serious about your work by being honest, responsible, and ethical. Once you prove yourself, you'll gain acceptance among your peers and be acknowledged as a valued part of the team. Resolve any conflicts in a professional manner.

13. **Hone your communications skills.** Ask questions and listen well. Continually strive to improve your writing abilities.

14. **Practice proper phone etiquette.** Answer your phone with a professional greeting; a simple "hello" just doesn't cut it in a work environment. You may want to ask your employer how to answer the phone, since different companies and positions within companies often have their own requirements. Be pleasant no matter how tired or exasperated you may be. Speak slowly and distinctly; do not mumble. When you place a call, be sure to identify yourself and to state your business in a clear manner.

    The office is not the place for personal calls. If you must make or receive an occasional personal call, keep it short and to the point.

15. **Watch your language.** Profanity and slang have no place in the business world. Learn office jargon and use it when appropriate. Focus on being clear in both your written communication and verbal communication. Remember, too, that any type of racial slur or a comment that could be perceived as sexual harassment is totally unacceptable. For any deviations from this policy, there are serious legal ramifications that go beyond being fired from your job. Remember, too, that employers have the technology and right to monitor your phone calls, voice mail, e-mail, and Internet activities.

16. **Behavior counts.** How you conduct yourself, how you interact with coworkers, and the way you approach your work will all affect your success. Superiors considering you for a promotion will usually take into account your work performance as well as how you deal with stress, how motivated you are, and how people like working with you.

17. **Act maturely.** Prove that you can work well without supervision and are dependable, responsible, and professional at all times.

18. **Keep your work space businesslike.** Offices can reflect the personalities of their occupants as long as the overall decor is not offensive or unprofessional. A few personal touches are fine: photos, diplomas, awards, and a few healthy plants. However, racy posters and calendars or posted slogans that reflect a negative attitude, such as "I love my job; it's the work I hate" or "Is it Friday yet?" should be avoided.

19. **Be organized.** Set up a filing system that works for you. If you don't have a system, ask a coworker for assistance, or get a book on developing organizational skills. The time you initially invest in getting organized will result in increased productivity. To avoid office clutter, you may want to set aside a few minutes at the beginning or end of each day to do housekeeping. Also take time to set daily, weekly, and long-term priorities.

20. **Stay informed.** Unlike school, where you were assigned reading material, on the job it's up to you to find and read material related to your position. Some of the material you might consider reading are industry trade journals and newsletters, competitors' sales literature, and a daily newspaper.

Don't forget to include the Internet in your research. Check the web regularly to see what's new and exciting in your field. Sites to include in your searches are those of professional associations in your field, competitors of your company, companies in related fields, and vendors to your industry.

21. **Be receptive to new ideas.** Be willing to learn new skills and new ways of doing specific tasks. When possible, take the ball and run with it.

22. **Keep your personal life personal.** Relationship problems and financial difficulties should be dealt with outside the office. Involving coworkers in personal problems is unprofessional.

23. **Learn to accept criticism.** Try not to become defensive when criticized. Instead, learn from your mistakes.

24. **Know your strengths and weaknesses.** What do you enjoy? What gives you a sense of satisfaction? What types of tasks make you uncomfortable? Position yourself to take on those responsibilities for which you are best suited.

25. **Write down short-term (daily, weekly, and monthly) and long-term (one-year, five-year, and ten-year) goals.** Make goals realistic and measurable. Evaluate yourself periodically. Revise goals when necessary.

26. **Accept all responsibilities graciously.** Realize that in your first job, you may be asked to do tasks that are entry level and may not fully utilize your education and skills. Complete those tasks with a good attitude, but seek opportunities to take on more challenging work.

27. **Accept the fact that you won't love every aspect of your job; few people do.** View each task as part of a bigger picture toward accomplishing your goals. Also, first jobs are just that—first jobs. Rarely does someone stay in a first job for life. Gain what you can out of the experience.

28. **Remember that you won't be new forever.** Eventually, you'll get to know the ropes just as your coworkers did. With a little enthusiasm, professionalism, and common sense, you'll be well on your way to success.

Tips for Working with Your Manager

Just as there are likable people and unlikable people, managers can fall into either category. If you're blessed with a good manager, you'll have the opportunity to learn from someone with experience and to develop a long-term professional relationship. If, on the other hand, you find getting along with your manager a challenge, swallow your pride and consider this an educational experience. Here are some tips for working with your manager:

1. **Understand your manager's position.** He or she must answer to another boss, who is interested only in performance and results. Be aware of your

manager's position relative to the company and your position relative to others whom he or she manages.

2. **Communicate with your manager.** As in any relationship, good communication is important. Don't be afraid to tell your manager of your successes, failures, and goals. He or she can't help you if you don't make known what you want.

3. **Take the ball and run with it.** Most managers would prefer to have their staff assume some responsibility without being micro-managed. Find ways to help your manager get the job done.

4. **Accept criticism without becoming defensive.** Work on improving deficiencies and learn from your mistakes.

5. **Consider the situation as short-term.** At some point in your career, you're likely to encounter someone with whom your personality clashes. If you see no hope for developing a good working relationship with your manager, begin quietly looking for your next job. Continue to act professionally and responsibly even if the situation gets rough. Finally, don't treat this glitch in your career as a personal failure. Instead, see it for what it is, learn from the experience, and move on.

INTERNET

If disagreements with your manager go beyond personality conflicts and you'd like to know more about your rights as an employee, check out www.disgruntled.com. It publishes complaints about employer mistreatment and outlines employee work-place rights.

Managing Relationships on the Job

KEY POINT

If you think that succeeding in a job depends wholly on your level of expertise and performance, you're mistaken. Good interpersonal skills can be just as important, if not more so. If your personal attributes and the culture of the hiring company don't merge, you may be in the wrong place. "Bad chemistry" is a mismatch with serious ramifications. If you can't adjust to the corporate culture—or it to you—you could be out of a job again.

The "right chemistry" is the behavioral style that fits in with the required style of the employer and of the particular job, in addition to the employee's having the requisite skills. Interpersonal characteristics and cultural fit are highly regarded assessments. Good social skills, a positive attitude, enthusiasm, and a sense of humor can be vital. Here are some other tips to help you establish successful relationships with your coworkers:

1. Develop relationships in which you have mutual respect. Mutual respect based on mutual gain is vital.

2. Learn to manage the small-group relationship. In school, you learned to work as an individual, but in companies, teamwork is the direction of the future.

3. Make a point of getting involved with other people in the organization and their work. Be friendly but not unproductive. It's good to have people on your side.

4. Upper management places high value on broad-based interpersonal and communication skills.

5. Ask everyone questions. Absorb information from all people. Be respectful of other people's jobs.

6. Pay attention to the actions and responses of others. Listen and observe. What are people saying and doing? Involve others in your day-to-day decisions.

7. Steer clear of office politics. How one deals with politics and other people is just as important as how well one does the job. It can greatly influence whether you succeed or fail.

8. Tips for Becoming a Team Player:

   a. Develop a "team mentality." Exhibit a good attitude.

   b. Participate in group activities both during company time and after hours. Sports such as softball and bowling can provide great bonding experiences. Social settings can help make work settings more comfortable, but remember that your conduct off-hours should never be inappropriate or fodder for the gossip mill.

   c. Show your team spirit; take pride in the team. Support your coworkers. Contribute to team success. Share credit for accomplishments, and congratulate others on their successes.

9. Traps to Avoid:

   a. Forming cliques. These little groups can make a statement to others that they don't belong. You could be alienating people whom you may one day need on your side.

   b. Sexual and racial comments. Sexual harassment and bigoted language are not acceptable, even behind closed doors.

   c. Passing judgment. Avoid being critical of others. Your judgments could be wrong, and your comments will most likely get back to you as the source.

   d. Kissing up to the boss. You'll alienate coworkers and eventually management if you take this tack. It's appropriate to let people know how you're doing but in the right forums, such as a monthly report.

e. Breaking a trust. This is the quickest way to lose friends in the work environment.

f. Gossiping. Talking about others is unprofessional. Talking about business issues outside work could be harmful to the business. Discretion is important. In business, gossip can get back to competitors, vendors, and suppliers. Be careful of what you say.

g. Socializing at work. Have fun, but strike a balance. Also, balance your work with your personal life. Being friends with only coworkers may be too much.

Finding a Mentor

KEY POINT

Find a good mentor, and you'll greatly accelerate your on-the-job learning and your potential for success. A mentor should be someone you respect, admire, and like. Mentors can set good examples, teach procedures, help you see the big picture, solve problems, guide you toward your future, give perspective, and provide emotional support. Women and minorities can especially benefit from mentoring, a system white males have used for years.

What's in the relationship for the mentor? Many professionals see mentoring as an opportunity to give back for their success. Some are flattered to have a new recruit admire them. Mentors also get the benefit of your loyalty and dedication. Your success may help translate into their success. They may look to you for help with special projects. You may also provide them with creativity, a new perspective in dealing with work situations.

To find a mentor, first identify someone with solid experience and good interpersonal skills. Some companies have an established mentoring program in which they will pair you with a willing coworker. Although it would be best to have a mentor within your own organization, you can also tap certain professional groups like SCORE, the Service Corps of Retired Executives. Be sensitive to your mentor's time. Then don't just take but find ways you can help that person do his or her job better. Recognize people's shortcomings while accepting their attributes. Appreciate that even mentors have a human side. Finally, when you eventually outgrow your mentor, don't forget who helped you get to that stage.

How You Will Be Evaluated

In school, you were accustomed to receiving midterm and final grades. In the real world, you'll most likely have performance reviews. The larger the company, the more formal the process tends to be. In essence, a performance review evaluates the quality of your work over a specific time period, usually a year.

Reviews are often a combination of objective and subjective criteria. They may look at how you've achieved short-term goals and progress made on long-term goals, as well as areas such as your attitude, ability to get along with others, and style of dress. Most likely, you will be rated with some form of grading system.

Usually, a performance review includes a salary review as well. Remember, raises in most companies are not guaranteed. Poor performance, rough times for the company, or management changes can all influence a potential raise. Try to focus on your contribution to the company as the reason for a raise. Your "need" for more money is not really relevant.

The most important part of a performance review should be a discussion of areas for improvement and the setting of new goals. Your task as an employee is to clarify any areas of your review that you're unsure of, accept constructive criticism with grace, and express a willingness to improve any trouble areas.

The Importance of Staying Current

KEY POINT

In today's fast-paced, competitive market, even when you have a job it is essential to stay current and informed. By continuing to improve your skills and education, you not only improve your job performance (and hopefully your compensation), but you also greatly enhance your marketability should you need to reenter the job hunt. Also, by keeping an active and curious mind you increase your job satisfaction and prevent burnout. Depending on your field, there are many avenues to self-improvement.

One of the most obvious ways to become more informed is through formal education. Take courses at your local college or your city's adult education program. Many colleges now cater to working adults by offering courses in the evenings or on weekends. It is also important to know that you do not have to complete a degree, but instead can dabble in a class or two to brush up on your writing, speaking, or computer skills. You will be surprised to see how many others like you are in your classes and how understanding most professors are regarding the needs of the working adult student. Returning to school can be a frightening experience for some, but most find the rewards well worth the initial apprehension.

In some cases, employers will team up with local educators and corporate trainers to design an appropriate course or seminar that could be offered right at your work place. This is something you may want to inquire about or suggest to your supervisor. Of course, if your employer already offers some additional training, you would be wise to jump at the opportunity.

There are other opportunities for formal education. Attend seminars and conferences sponsored by your local professional organizations or trade associations. These seminars are often specifically designed to meet a need common to people in your profession. They tend to be brief, focused, and highly informational—a good choice for those with little time. Moreover, all the places where education or training occur offer another hidden but invaluable asset: the opportunity to network and learn about the technology and news in your field through word of mouth. Avoid the temptation to be a wallflower or to take a wait-and-see attitude. You may learn more by making small talk with the person next to you in the coffee line than you ever thought possible.

A more formal way to guarantee the benefits of networking is by joining networking groups. These groups usually meet once a month and allow members the opportunity to exchange business cards, develop contacts, keep track of developments in the field, and get to know their competitors.

Other ways to keep on top of important developments in your field while networking include joining trade associations or professional organizations. Virtually every profession has a national association that offers a publication on developments in the field, as well as updates on relevant legislation and technology. Even if you choose not to join your national or local professional or trade organization, it is still a good idea to check out these publications at your local library. When considering whether you should become involved, keep in mind that trade and professional organizations typically offer discounted student memberships and are often looking for leadership at the local or national levels.

These same organizations also offer trade shows where leaders in the field meet to show off their latest products and rub elbows. You may find that after attending a few trade shows you begin to recognize the names and faces of key industry players. They, in turn, may even get to know you!

There are also other opportunities for staying current that might not initially come to mind. Some people choose to get an inside look at a particular type of business by doing temporary, freelance, or consulting work. Others choose to go straight to the source and ask for informational interviews of people in the industry. (See page 70 for tips on how to conduct informational interviews.)

Finally, it is important to remember to keep an open and curious mind. Read newspapers and relevant magazines to keep abreast of larger trends and issues that affect your field. Search the Internet on a regular basis for news on your field, related businesses, and your employer's competitors and vendors. Offer to cross-train at your place of employment or to assist your coworkers whenever you're able. By continuing the lifelong process of listening and learning, you will find that you have become a much sought-after and indispensable member of the work force.

Alternative Work Arrangements

Changing social values have resulted in employees demanding a more diverse array of work options to fit their lifestyles. A number of factors are contributing to this trend:

1. There are an increasing number of single-parent families.

2. More professional women want to raise their children while continuing in their careers.

3. Older employees wish to postpone retirement but reduce their working hours.

4. Employees are more conscious of the amount of time they spend commuting.

5. American workers are placing more value on personal time.

6. More workers want to continue their education while employed.

You may find that one of these situations applies to you. Five types of work arrangements are most common:

Standard work schedule.   Based on a forty-hour work week, this is the most common schedule. The forty hours usually does not include lunchtime. The typical business begins its day at 8:30 A.M. or 9:00 A.M. and is open until 5:00 P.M. or 5:30 P.M., Monday through Friday. However, many businesses may start at different hours; construction companies often start their day quite early, and restaurants may not open until 10:00 A.M.

Flextime.   This type of schedule gives employees a choice of work hours. Some may prefer to start work early and finish early, whereas others may prefer to start work later and finish later. Employees are thus able to gear their schedules to optimum commuting times or child care arrangements. *Core time* represents the hours each day the employees are required to be at work, and employees select which of the remaining hours they prefer. In all, each employee must work a forty-hour week.

Job sharing.   In job sharing, two people divide the responsibilities of a regular full-time job. This type of arrangement is becoming more common, especially among women who wish to spend time at home with their children while continuing to work at their profession.

Compressed work week.   By extending the workday beyond the standard eight hours, employees can create a schedule in which they work the required forty hours in a three- or four-day week.

Telecommuting.   With advances in technology, more people are able to avoid time-consuming commutes by operating out of their homes or satellite offices some, if not all, of their workdays. Telecommuters keep in touch with coworkers by phone, fax, modem, and e-mail. In theory, by using a laptop computer and cell phone, employees can set up a virtual office anywhere.

When to Move On

Whether your first job is the best thing that ever happened to you or just so-so, there will probably come a time when you should consider exploring new opportunities. That time may come after a few months, several years, or more. How do you know when you're ready? Take this short test:

1. I feel dissatisfied with my job.   ❑ yes   ❑ no

2. I argue frequently with my boss.   ❑ yes   ❑ no

3. I feel stifled in my position.   ❑ yes   ❑ no

4. I no longer feel challenged.   ❑ yes   ❑ no

5. I am not compensated fairly for my work.   ❑ yes   ❑ no

If you answered yes to any of these questions, you may want to think about moving on. Before taking action, consider the following variables:

1. Are there other opportunities in my field?   ❑ yes   ❑ no

2. Would I have to relocate to find a new job?   ❑ yes   ❑ no

3. Do I have enough experience to obtain a better position?   ❑ yes   ❑ no

4. Are there perks on this job that would be hard to replace, such as health care benefits, flexible hours, or a convenient commute?   ❑ yes   ❑ no

A job can easily turn into a security blanket for you. You are comfortable with your responsibilities and you know and like your coworkers. It's up to you to decide if those are good reasons to stay. Taking risks can be scary, but it often results in the biggest gains.

DIVE IN

Try to best explore your opportunities before leaving your current job. You can negotiate from a stronger position if you already have a job. Be discreet about your new job search, and be professional if you do decide to leave. Try not to burn any bridges. Give at least two weeks notice to your employer, and try not to leave any projects unfinished. You'll want your old employer to remember you favorably should you ever need a recommendation.

Planning Your Future

Trends in the Work Force

The twenty-first century will see dramatic changes in the U.S. labor force and economy. Knowing some of the trends may help you better plan your future:

1. There will be a shortage of competent workers with basic literacy and learning skills.

2. A renewed and strong U.S. manufacturing sector will create few new jobs due to automation and streamlined operations. Of the manufacturing jobs created, most will be in sales and marketing.

3. Service industries will be responsible for most of the job growth in the next decade.

4. Government efforts to reduce unemployment will continue to target the unskilled and poor.

5. As baby boomers reach middle age and as the U.S. birthrate continues at near zero-population growth, fewer young people will be available for entry-level positions. Businesses will either recruit and train more of the hardcore unemployed, unskilled, and elderly, or will automate. On the plus side, people who lose their jobs or are considering changing careers will be able to find more stopgap job opportunities in entry-level positions.

6. Women, Hispanics, Asians, other minorities, and older workers will significantly increase their representation in the labor market. The proportion of white men, young people, African Americans, and non-Hispanic whites, while growing, will become a smaller share of the labor force by 2005.

7. More immigrants will enter the United States, both documented and undocumented, to meet labor shortages at all levels. Developing countries will continue to experience a brain drain as trained professionals emigrate to North America.

8. High-paying jobs will grow faster than low-paying jobs. Sixty percent of new jobs will offer above-average wages.

9. Part-time and temporary employment opportunities will increase as more companies attempt to lower personnel costs as well as achieve greater personnel flexibility by minimizing the size of their full-time permanent staff.

10. More clerical and service jobs will become available in response to new information technologies.

11. Professionals will need to have more technical skills to succeed in the age of information technology.

12. The population as well as wealth and economic activity will continue to shift into the Northwest, Southwest, and Florida at the expense of the Northeast

and north central regions. People will gravitate to communities with job opportunities.

13. Employees increasingly will work outside their company offices—possibly from other states—as reliance on communication via technology increases.

14. As we move into a world economy, opportunities will abound for professionals willing to relocate abroad, particularly if they are proficient in languages.

15. As many large companies cut back their work force, and as more people decide to experiment with changing careers, more small businesses will be started as entrepreneurs capitalize on new opportunities in the high-tech and service areas. Estimates are that an additional 950,000 workers will choose self-employment.

16. Opportunities for career advancement will be increasingly limited within most organizations due to a focus on nonhierarchical forms of organization, the burgeoning managerial ranks, and the postponement of retirement by baby boomers.

17. More people will use job hopping as a method for advancement and career stimulation.

18. Benefit packages will decline as health care costs continue to rise and organizations seek to minimize personnel expenses.

19. Job satisfaction will become less oriented toward advancement up the organizational ladder and more toward organization perks such as club memberships, vacations, sabbaticals, retraining opportunities, flexible work hours, family services, and health care packages.

EXERCISE

Discussion Questions

EXERCISE

1. Can you describe some of the differences between the working world of today and that of your parents? Your grandparents?

2. How do you think the working world will differ when your children embark on their careers?

3. Do you think most of the changes in the job market in the last twenty to fifty years have been positive or negative?

4. What changes/trends would you like to see in the future?

Sources: Bureau of Labor Statistics, *The Occupational Outlook Handbook.*

■ Top Careers in the Twenty-first Century

Should you modify your studies based on predictions of what jobs will be hot in the next ten years? Probably not—however, this doesn't mean you should ignore the valuable information that job market forecasts can provide.

The Occupational Outlook Handbook, published by the federal government, is an excellent job research tool. It is filled with data on occupational trends from the Bureau of Labor Statistics. It includes series reports, research papers, and economic studies on employment as well as listings of career materials and job resources.

In its forecast of job trends through 2005, it predicts enormous growth in the following five occupations: engineering and computer technology, business and financial services, health care, information technology, and biotechnology and science. The need for teachers and human services workers will also surge in the next ten years. Does your chosen career fall into any of these categories? If not, don't despair. The *Handbook* points out that while the greatest growth will be in high-tech industries, the majority of jobs will continue to be in the traditional service businesses such as retail, construction, finance, and real estate.

A more telling indication of where jobs of the future may lie is in the direct correlation that the Bureau of Labor Statistics makes between the growth potential for a vocation and how much education and training it requires. Growth rates through 2005 will range from 5 percent for occupations generally requiring moderate on-the-job training to 29 percent for occupations requiring a master's degree. All jobs requiring an associate degree or more are expected to grow about 15 percent.

The common factor in obtaining a good job—one that will position you for the broadest opportunity, the best salary and benefits, and the greatest security—is advanced education and training.

Whereas *The Occupational Outlook Handbook* provides information for the nation as a whole, there are other resources that can help you find state and local-area information. State occupational information coordinating committees can provide you with information directly or refer you to other specific sources. The state employment security agencies develop detailed information about local labor markets, such as current and projected employment by occupation and industry characteristics of the work force, and changes in state and local-area economic activity. You can get phone numbers for these agencies in the government pages of your local phone book.

■ Fast-Growing Occupations

Combine a shrinking labor force with a rapidly expanding global economy and what do you get? Oodles of opportunity for job seekers. About twenty million new jobs are expected to be created in the next five years. The computer and health care industries will see lots of growth. As the technology revolution continues and the baby boomers push toward old age, demand for skilled personnel will be huge in both areas.

In fields such as teaching and police work, legions of people with decades of expertise are getting ready to retire, creating numerous openings. Of course, despite the generally rosy outlook for many workers, some occupations, such as farming and manufacturing, will see little or no growth.

HOT JOBS

The fastest-growing occupations, 1996–2006, according to the Labor Department.

Occupation	Pct. Change
Database administrators, computer-support specialists, and all other computer scientists	118%
Computer engineers	109
Systems analysts	103
Personal- and home-care aides	85
Physical- and corrective-therapy assistants and aides	79
Home health aides	76
Medical assistants	74
Desktop publishing specialists	74
Physical therapists	71
Occupational therapy assistants and aides	69
Paralegals	68
Occupational therapists	66
Teachers, special education	59
Human services workers	55
Data-processing equipment repairers	52

Source: U.S. Department of Labor

SOME FAST-GROWING OCCUPATIONS AND THEIR SALARIES	
Occupation	**Approximate Yearly Salary**
Physical therapy assistant	$30,000
Occupational therapy assistant	$27,442
Dietitian	$31,300
Dental hygienist	$39,468
Medical assistant	$16,785–$22,672
Electroneurodiagnostic technologist	$26,800
Radiology technician	$29,300
Paralegal	$28,800
Human services worker	$15,000–$25,000
Teacher's aide	$18,803
Child care worker	$9,880–$16,120
Science technician (chemical, biological)	$19,800–$37,100
Engineering technician	$17,700–$22,800
Source: U.S. Department of Labor, Bureau of Labor Statistics, 1999	

■ The Unsung Benefits of the Two-Year Degree

Many students are unaware of the benefits of their two-year degree. Consider the following:*

- In 1998, more than ten million people—one out of every eighteen adults—were enrolled in a community college.

- The average expected lifetime earnings for a graduate with an associate's degree is more than $1 million. (That's a quarter of a million more than an individual with only a high school diploma.)

- Of all the jobs that were created between 1984 and 2000, more than half required some education beyond high school. Twenty-two percent will require one to three years of college.

- In recent surveys of employers in all hiring sectors—service, manufacturing, and nonprofit—more than half of respondents said that they will hire two-year graduates. Most likely to be hired: those in the fields of manufacturing and industrial equipment, finance, accounting, business, computer science and technology, and liberal arts.

---

*Source: National Association of Colleges and Employers, 1999; Bureau of Labor Statistics, 1999.

- Many associate-degree graduates have previous work experience—a big plus with today's employer.

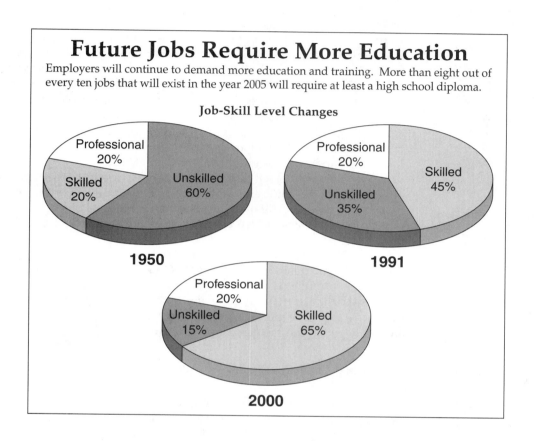

Future Jobs Require More Education

Employers will continue to demand more education and training. More than eight out of every ten jobs that will exist in the year 2005 will require at least a high school diploma.

Job-Skill Level Changes

Professional 20%
Skilled 20%
Unskilled 60%
1950

Professional 20%
Skilled 45%
Unskilled 35%
1991

Professional 20%
Unskilled 15%
Skilled 65%
2000

■ Job Security—A Thing of the Past?

In your grandparents' and parents' generations, job security was almost a given. You worked hard for a company, and in return for your loyalty the company provided you with a secure job through to your retirement. Times certainly have changed. Today, changing jobs every few years, either by choice or by necessity, is much more common. Even in good times, companies "downsize" to reduce overhead, merge with other companies to enhance their competitive position and then reorganize their work force, and adopt new technologies that enable fewer people to do more work.

The good news is that although companies are increasingly quick to lay off employees, stable jobs haven't completely disappeared. They survive because company success often depends on experienced workers. Turnover is costly to companies. Seasoned workers know a company's products, policies, and customers. New workers require training. And there's no guarantee that once trained, a new worker will have what it takes to fit in or succeed.

In many ways, job insecurity is greater than actual job loss. Blue-collar workers, the unskilled, and new recruits have always experienced a certain level of insecurity about their jobs. But now that insecurity has spread, amid much media attention, to managers, professionals, and upper-income workers who previously felt protected. Fortunately, job loss is not as bad as the headlines would have us believe. The economy still creates a steady stream of new jobs to replace those that are lost. And most fired workers, about 75 percent according to the U.S. Department of Labor, do get new jobs (albeit not always at the same salary level). An additional 14 percent, concentrated among workers older than fifty-five, retire. Only about 11 percent are still unemployed two years after being fired.

In a competitive economy, companies that can't minimize their payroll expenses won't survive, but neither will those that are so ruthless that they demoralize their workers and can't attract good new recruits. The bottom line is that most companies can still offer at least a moderate level of job security, but we'll never return to the post-Depression days when your first job could well be your job for life.

As a job hunter, you'll want to seek out companies that have a reputation for fairness and are positioned for growth. Once you obtain a position, you'll want to keep your résumé updated, stay informed about companies and trends in your field, and continue networking in your industry. That way, if you're ever a victim of downsizing or corporate restructuring, you'll have the elements in place to smoothly go to your next career opportunity.

◼ Where Do Jobs Come From?

When considering what job openings there will be in the years to come, it is important to understand where new jobs come from. Jobs are created through replacement, people who have left their old jobs for various reasons, or from growth, new openings created by the employer.

- Growth accounts for 38 percent of all job openings.

- Replacement accounts for 62 percent of all job openings.

Projected openings by major occupational group, in millions, 1994–2005:

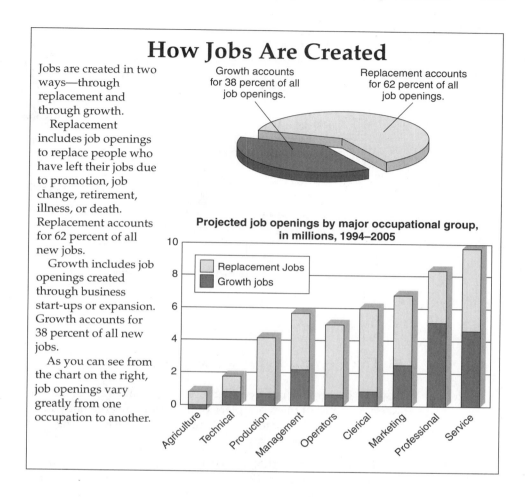

How Jobs Are Created

Jobs are created in two ways—through replacement and through growth.

Replacement includes job openings to replace people who have left their jobs due to promotion, job change, retirement, illness, or death. Replacement accounts for 62 percent of all new jobs.

Growth includes job openings created through business start-ups or expansion. Growth accounts for 38 percent of all new jobs.

As you can see from the chart on the right, job openings vary greatly from one occupation to another.

Growth accounts for 38 percent of all job openings.

Replacement accounts for 62 percent of all job openings.

Projected job openings by major occupational group, in millions, 1994–2005

Replacement Jobs
Growth jobs

Agriculture · Technical · Production · Management · Operators · Clerical · Marketing · Professional · Service

■ A Changing Work Force

Considering how tight the labor market is now, it's hard to believe that the balance of power could shift even further in employees' favor. The fast-changing global economy and advances in technology are going to play a big role in creating new employment opportunities. It is expected that there will be too few workers for too many openings.

It's not hard to see why. For decades the seventy-six million baby boomers—now thirty-five to fifty-three years old—have crowded the work place. But as this population ages there won't be enough Generation Xers, those now age twenty-three to thirty-four, and Echo Boomers, members of the so-called Generation Y, now age five to twenty-two, to take their place. As baby boomers retire, employers will be hard pressed to fill the gap.

Crunch Time

The 25–to–44 work force will shrink nearly 12 percent over the decade ending in 2006. The change in work force by age group over each time frame:

How the ratio of people ages 20 to 64 to people age 65 and older will shrink in coming decades:

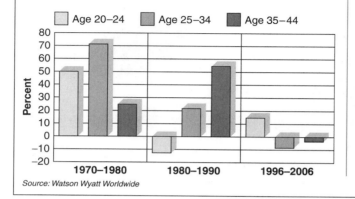

Source: Watson Wyatt Worldwide

Year	Ratio
1955	6.29 to 1
1990	4.69 to 1
2010	4.47 to 1
2030	2.65 to 1
2050	2.59 to 1

Source: Sylvester Schieber and John Shoven

■ The New Rules for Career Success

Today's highly competitive job market has changed the rules for career success. Keeping up with the work place of the future means that you'll have to keep learning and be ready to adapt to new ideas. The following are some of the basic premises that have emerged:

1. **Get computer skills.** Even the most routine job today requires some knowledge of computers. Fortunately, today's computers are more user friendly than ever before, so don't be intimidated. You needn't be familiar with the myriad of programs on the market today, but you should have a functional understanding of word processing, spreadsheets, database management, and any applications specific to your career field. You don't have to become a "computer wizard" to prosper in the work force. The real issue is one of comfort.

2. **Keep learning.** Now that you either have your college degree or are about to get it you may think that you're through with your education. The fact is that "what you earn depends on what you learn." Although your education may provide some competitive edge today, you'll need to keep sharpening that edge for a future payoff. Read the trade journals in your field, take courses, and go to trade shows to stay current. The most important thing you may take away from your college education is not what you learned but rather that you learned how to learn.

HOW THE JOB MARKET IS CHANGING			
	1994	**2005***	**Change**
The labor force is growing:			
The civilian labor force	131 million	147 million	+12%
The labor force is a diverse group:			
White	77%	72%	−5%
Black	12%	13%	+1%
Hispanic	9%	11%	+2%
Asian and others	4%	6%	+2%
Women are continuing to join the labor force:			
Women participating in the labor force	59%	62%	+3%
Women as a percentage of the labor force	46%	48%	+2%
We are a nation of service providers:			
Jobs producing goods	24 mil.	23 mil.	−1%
Jobs producing services	89 mil.	107 mil.	+20%
The labor force is getting older:			
Workers aged 16 to 24 years	22 mil.	23 mil.	+1%
Workers aged 25 to 34 years	34 mil.	31 mil.	−9%
Workers aged 35 to 44 years	35 mil.	36 mil.	+3%
Workers aged 45 to 54 years	24 mil.	35 mil.	+45%
Workers aged 55 years and older	16 mil.	22 mil.	+39%
Education pays:	**Mean Annual Wage**	**Simple Forty-Year Earnings**	
Not a high school graduate	$13,800	$552,000	
High school graduate	$20,200	$808,000	
Associate or technical degree	$23,200	$928,000	
Bachelor's degree	$37,200	$1,488,000	
Advanced degree	$56,100	$2,244,000	

*Projections

3. **Hone your general business skills.** Knowing how to write and speak effectively will help you succeed in any job. Work toward continual improvement by reading books, learning from others, and practicing skills. Time management, organizational skills, and the ability to build relationships are also vital to career success at any level.

Once you have your college degree, it's important to stay current in your field. In the twenty-first century, what you earn will depend on what you learn. (© Rachel Epstein/ PhotoEdit)

4. **Forget about climbing; start spinning.** Think of a career less as a ladder to climb and more like a web to spin. Webs have a center but no top, and a lot of paths that connect. Today, most people find that they spiral from job to job, sometimes in the same company, sometimes between companies. They stay within a general field, but that field has no sharp borders. Forget the climb— move along webs, earning more from the skills you gained, not seniority. The result? In addition to success, you'll have a much more interesting life.

5. **Networking works.** The best way to refine your skills and widen your web is by networking. Networking is no longer just for exchanging information about job openings, but rather a means of actively connecting with people throughout your industry and profession. It is a way to keep current. Information is the key to the future in any field.

6. **Join the team.** Most of today's companies are organizing themselves internally by teams. Teammates at work may know one another only by phone,

fax, or Internet address, but they are still interdependent. The academic world is geared to reward individual performances. As you enter the work world, prepare to make the transition to working in groups. Develop skills that involve dividing responsibility, respecting the knowledge of others, and sharing credit for accomplishments.

CHAPTER
17

You Can Do It!

Success Stories

Following is a sampling of how some of the people we interviewed for *The Ultimate Job Hunter's Guidebook* found their jobs. The answers vary from simply responding to a classified ad, to creatively transferring skills in one area to another, to aggressive networking combined with a stroke of good luck. By telling you their stories, we hope you'll be inspired by their success and moved to action in getting your own career off the ground.

"I was attending classes during the day to become a paralegal and waitressing at night just to pay my bills. One of the regulars happened to be a partner in a prominent law firm. We became friends, and he gave me my first paralegal job."

Ilene
Paralegal

"I sent a cover letter and my résumé to a major advertising agency in my area asking if they had any openings for a copywriter. They sent me a form rejection letter. About two weeks later I got a call from that agency's largest client, a major cruise line, seeking an in-house promotions writer. The agency had passed my résumé along. I had a brief interview with the manager, who hired me on the spot, saying the recommendation from the ad agency was all she needed to make her decision."

Jennifer
Promotions Writer

"My roommate heard a radio station advertising for sales representatives. She called to request an interview. By the time the radio station returned her call several weeks later, she had accepted another position. I took her interview and got the job."

Jamie
Radio Sales Account Executive

"I did clerical temporary work at a tourist bureau while I was job hunting for a marketing position. The tourist bureau had no full-time openings. However, the vice president for whom I worked soon left the company to start his own marketing consulting business. He hired me to be his right-hand man."

Paul
Marketing Consultant

"For years I was a nurse in a major hospital. I got to know many of the sales representatives from the pharmaceutical companies. I let one of the reps know I was looking to get out of nursing. I gave her a copy of my résumé, which she passed along to her sales manager, who eventually hired me."

Karen
Pharmaceutical Sales Representative

"I was flying home for the holidays, depressed that I still hadn't found a job. When I boarded the plane, I found someone already sitting in my seat. As it turned out, her

last name was the same as mine, hence the seat mixup. I ended up taking the seat next to her, and we chatted the entire flight. I told her I was seeking a position as a product manager with a manufacturer. She worked for a major employer in my area and gave me the names of people to contact and also some inside information about the company's anticipated growth. Her tips were right on the money, and I had a job within a month."

Candy
Product Manager

"To keep busy when I was job hunting, I helped my dad set up a web page on the Internet for his company. He got so many compliments on it that some of his friends asked me to help design web pages for their businesses. Before I knew it, I was in business."

Daniel
Internet Designer

"The human resources department of a health care company had me interview for the position of respiratory therapist. After the first few minutes of the interview, the human resources representative sent me directly to the respiratory department manager, who would ultimately make the hiring decision. The manager was furious when I knocked at his door. He resented that human resources had not contacted him properly to schedule the interview. He was rude to me and spent the entire meeting fuming at the situation. After the meeting I was extremely upset, but decided to send the manager a gracious thank-you note anyway. Two days later he called to say he'd received my note. He apologized for his inappropriate behavior and offered me the job."

Jan
Respiratory Therapist

"I wanted to be a police officer from the time I could talk. When I was in high school, I worked at an amusement park during my summer vacation. One summer vacation from college, where I was majoring in law enforcement, I was moved into the security department at the amusement park and eventually promoted to head of security. My years at the park combined with my law enforcement degree helped me easily land my dream job as a police officer."

Todd
Police Officer

"When my three children were young, it was always a challenge to find good domestic help. I was constantly searching for the perfect nanny, a quality housekeeper, a mother's helper. After a while, I realized that many of my friends were asking me to use my experience and research to help them find domestic help. That's how I began my domestic employment agency, now in its eleventh year of business."

Rosie
Owner, domestic employment agency

"I studied marketing at college, but skiing is my real love. Fortunately, I was able to find a job that combined the two. I'm a marketing director for an upscale ski resort."

Gary
Marketing Director

"I applied for an entry-level public relations job at a nonprofit organization that I had seen posted at my college. I was granted an interview, which involved a two-hour drive from my home. When I got to the interview, I learned that the person I was to meet had called in sick, and no one had thought to cancel my interview. One of her co-workers, feeling badly about the miscommunication, offered to interview me in her stead. We hit it off, and he recommended me for the job. I later learned that his recommendation was so strong that no one else was even interviewed."

Tracey
Public Relations Coordinator

"I graduated with a degree in art but couldn't find a job in my field. I went to work in a local bakery as a cake decorator. Customers would often compliment me on my unique, artistic cake designs. One customer asked if I ever did any painting. When I told her my degree was in art, she hired me to paint a mural on her child's bedroom wall. She loved the work and began passing my name around to her many friends. I was hired to do everything from painting family portraits to designing custom Christmas cards. While I still can't wholly support myself on my artwork, my business is slowly growing, and I hope to one day work full-time as an artist."

Marty
Artist

"I had answered an ad for a human resources representative for a major tourist attraction. I had three lengthy interviews over the course of a month. In the end, another candidate was selected. I was extremely disappointed because I had invested a lot of time and been confident I would be chosen. Nonetheless, I sent notes to the people who'd interviewed me, thanking them for their consideration. I was glad I did, because three weeks later the company called me back. They had another opening, and it was mine if I wanted it."

Ronnie
Human Resources Representative

"I saw an ad in the paper seeking a creative marketing person for a software development company. I decided to try something a bit off-the-wall. I shipped my résumé in a big box along with a beach ball that had my name and phone number scrawled on it. In my cover letter I explained that I was the type of person who could 'take the ball and run with it.' I got the interview and the job. And to this day, staff people in the human resources department can sometimes be caught playing beach ball with my 'application.'"

Avi
Vice President, Marketing

"I had always dreamed of working in a museum. I frequented our local museum and became friends with one of the researchers. When she mentioned she was leaving to take another position, I applied for her job. With her recommendation, I was easily hired."

Phillip
Museum Researcher

"I saw a job advertised for a reporter for a small weekly newspaper. Because I wanted the job so badly, I kept calling the publisher. I must have called four times a day for three weeks until he finally agreed to meet with me. Eventually, he hired me. He said someone as persistent as I had been had to be a good reporter."

Steven
Reporter

Success Story

Can you guess who? . . .

Failed in business	age 22
Ran for legislature and was defeated	age 23
Again failed in business	age 24
Elected to legislature	age 25
Sweetheart died	age 26
Had a nervous breakdown	age 27
Defeated for Speaker	age 29
Defeated for Congress	age 34
Elected to Congress	age 37
Defeated for Congress	age 39
Defeated for Senate	age 46
Defeated for Vice President	age 47
Defeated for Senate	age 49
Elected President of the United States	age 51

That man was Abraham Lincoln.

"While I was a senior in college I did volunteer work at the local chapter of the United Way. I got to know many of the staff people. When I graduated, they used their contacts to help me get a full-time position as an accountant with one of the agencies the United Way supports."

Mandy
Accountant

"I had been seeking a position as an administrative assistant for several months. To help pay the bills but keep my days open for interviews, I worked nights cleaning of-

fices. One of the offices I cleaned belonged to a law firm, and I became friendly with a couple of the lawyers who worked late. They helped me get an interview at their firm when a position became available. Now someone cleans my office."

Leah
Administrative Assistant

"I volunteered as a reporter for my college newspaper. One of the stories I wrote was about credit card fraud, and I interviewed several bankers in my area for information. I made sure they each received a copy of the article when it was published, along with a thank-you note for their time. Two months later when I graduated, I contacted these bankers again to let them know I was seeking a job in the banking industry. One of them had an opening in his bank's credit card division and referred me for the job."

Sharon
Credit Analyst

"For years I stayed home taking care of my four young children. When the youngest started school, I felt lost. I wanted to work but didn't know what kind of job I could do. It had been years since I had held a paying job. Fortunately, I was able to convince an employer that my caregiving skills—organizational, creativity, and patience—were 'transferable' to the type of position she needed to fill."

Linda
Activities Director for a nursing home

"I was seeking an entry-level position with an engineering firm. The owner of one of the companies I applied to was an alumnus of my college and interviewed me out of respect for his alma mater. We hit it off, and he hired me."

Ross
Engineer

"I wrote a term paper my senior year about child abuse. As part of my research, I interviewed several social workers. When I graduated, one of them helped me get a wonderful job in a child psychologist's office."

Thomas
Behavioral Therapist

"When I was growing up, my family was very interested in the stock market. I learned a great deal about investing. I went to college for accounting and found that my knowledge of the financial markets came in handy. I had no problem combining the two into a career."

Dawn
Financial Planner

"I was looking for a computer programming position. While job searching, I managed to obtain a couple of freelance programming jobs, which then led to additional work. Before I knew it, I was working full-time as an independent programmer. I *hadn't even considered self-employment. Now I don't think I would ever consider working for someone else."*

Sherry
Computer Programmer

"My mother always made the best apple pies. When I graduated college and was home trying to find work as a sales representative, I came up with the idea of selling Mom's pies. I would go to local food stores and specialty shops and convince them to carry our product. The pies really started selling, and orders began coming in. Now both Mom and I have full-time jobs."

John
Apple Pie Salesperson

"I had worked as a secretary for about five years. I knew I was ready for a new challenge but didn't know what direction to go. Then I became pregnant. At one of my obstetrical visits, I was given an ultrasound test, which allowed me to see the fetus moving around in my belly. I found it fascinating. After I had the baby, I began attending night school to become an ultrasound technician. Now I get to share the joy of others seeing their babies for the first time."

Lisa
Ultrasound Technician

"During my college summer vacations, I volunteered at a local animal shelter. In addition to some great experience, I got to know all the local veterinarians. When I graduated, a veterinarian who remembered me from the shelter offered me a job."

Ken
Veterinary Assistant

"I interviewed with an editor of a small weekly newspaper to be a freelance writer. While we chatted, he mentioned that the publisher was planning to start a new magazine targeted at women. He introduced me to the publisher, and within a week I was hired full-time as editor."

Maureen
Magazine Editor

"I was always very overweight. In college I decided to do something about it. I began going to a nutritionist for counseling. I became so interested in the field, I changed my major from nursing to nutrition and eventually went to work at the practice where I first learned how to manage my own weight problem."

Patti
Nutritionist

"I had applied for numerous teaching jobs using conventional methods and been unsuccessful. One day, in a fit of desperation, I walked into a local college, located the chairperson for the English department, and hastily explained why I would be an ex-

cellent candidate for her next open position. She agreed, and as luck would have it, had an opening. I walked out with a job offer in less than twenty minutes."

Melissa
English Professor

"*In high school I worked in a motorcycle parts store nights and weekends. My boss really liked me, and told me that there would always be a place for me in his company. I went to college and majored in management. When I graduated, I called my old boss. By then his business had grown to four stores. He hired me to oversee his entire operation.*"

James
Operations Manager

"*I interviewed for a position as a buyer for a major retailer. In the course of our conversation the interviewer happened to mention that he loved jellybeans. The next day I sent him a bag of gourmet jellybeans along with a thank-you note, mentioning how I'd been able to find this unique product for a great price, and I looked forward to applying those skills in my next job. I got the position, and to this day keep a jar of jellybeans on my desk.*"

Robin
Retail Buyer

"*I began as an administrative assistant for a property management company. Initially, my work involved mostly clerical tasks, but as the business grew and we acquired more clients, I took on more property management responsibilities. I began taking night courses in real estate management. Soon after that I was promoted to property manager and had to hire my own administrative assistant.*"

Judy
Property Manager

"*I studied to become a teacher, but when I graduated, no jobs were available at local schools. Reading the classified ads one day, I saw several positions advertised for corporate training associates. I found I had most of the required skills and decided to apply. Now I work for a large computer company 'teaching' new hires our policies and procedures.*"

Stephen
Corporate Training Associate

"*I studied dance performance all through college. After graduation, I went to numerous auditions and soon learned that there were many more dancers than there were positions available. Eventually I was able to get a job that kept me involved in the dance profession and also helped me develop management expertise. I became a performance coordinator for a traveling dance company.*"

Carol
Dance Performance Coordinator

"I was a customer service representative for the local telephone company. With increased automation, the company was experiencing numerous layoffs, and for my position the writing was on the wall. I contacted the local electric company and was immediately hired because of my experience working for a utility company."

Tom
Customer Service Representative

"I placed a positions wanted ad in an advertising trade journal for an electronic art specialist. I got calls from ad agencies, a couple of companies with in-house graphics departments, and a statewide newspaper. I chose the newspaper because it seemed to present the most opportunity for long-term growth."

David
Electronic Art Specialist

The Victor, by C. W. Longenecker

If you think you are beaten, you are.
If you think you dare not, you don't.
If you like to win but think you can't,
It's almost a cinch you won't.
If you think you'll lose, you're lost.
For out in the world we find
Success begins with a fellow's will.
It's all in the state of mind.
If you think you are outclassed, you are.
You've got to think high to rise.
You've got to be sure of yourself before
You can ever win the prize.
Life's battles don't always go
To the stronger or faster man.
But sooner or later, the man who wins
Is the man who thinks he can.

"We moved around a lot for my husband's job, and I became quite skilled at buying and selling houses. I eventually got my real estate license and became a real estate salesperson."

Irene
Realtor

"After college graduation, I interned in the news department at a local TV station. I was envious of my friends who were making big money while I was essentially a volunteer, but I knew my time would come. I spent most days in the sports department. Because it was understaffed, I was frequently given reporting assignments that

might otherwise have gone to more seasoned reporters. Eventually, the sports department was given the budget to expand. I was hired full-time as a sports reporter and am currently working toward becoming a sports anchor."

Dan
Sports Reporter

Failures Who Became Successes

Gain inspiration and motivation from these "failures."

- Albert Einstein was 4 years old before he could speak.

- Isaac Newton did poorly in grade school and was considered "unpromising."

- Beethoven's music teacher once said of him, "As a composer, he is hopeless."

- When Thomas Edison was a youngster, his teacher told him he was too stupid to learn anything. He was counseled to go into a field where he might succeed by virtue of his pleasant personality.

- F. W. Woolworth got a job in a dry goods store when he was 21, but his employer would not permit him to wait on customers because he "didn't have enough sense to close a sale."

- Michael Jordan was cut from his high school basketball team.

- Boston Celtics Hall of Famer Bob Cousy suffered the same fate.

- A newspaper editor fired Walt Disney because he "lacked imagination and had no good ideas."

- Winston Churchill failed the sixth grade and had to repeat it because he did not complete the tests that were required for promotion.

- Babe Ruth struck out 1,300 times—a major league record.

"I had studied liberal arts in college and wasn't quite sure exactly what career I was going to pursue. I joined a club of women entrepreneurs for the purposes of networking and learning what types of careers other women had. I became friends with a woman who owned a secretarial school. One day she mentioned that she was in a jam because her communications skills teacher had just quit, and classes were scheduled to start in three days. Since I was unemployed and felt I had good communications skills, I offered to substitute until she could find a replacement. The first class went so well, she offered me the job full-time. I love it!"

Diane
Teacher

"I studied cosmetology in my home country, Germany. After I immigrated to the United States, I learned that a company that manufactured a line of cosmetics I liked was planning to expand into this country. I contacted them, explained my familiarity with their products and knowledge of the American market, and was hired as a marketing consultant. Eventually, I was promoted to vice president of the North American division of the company."

Inge
Vice President, cosmetics company

"I am a stay-at-home mom. One day when my kids were napping, I painted a floral design on a watering can I had in my garage. My mother-in-law happened to see it when visiting and asked if I could make some more for her upcoming garden club crafts fair. I painted seventeen watering cans, and they all sold. Then I began painting on all kinds of objects from glass vases to ceramic planters. I now sell my works to about a dozen retail establishments in my area. The painting gives me a creative outlet and an income while allowing me scheduling flexibility to remain a full-time mother."

Sophie
Artist

"I was about to graduate with a degree in architectural engineering technology when I came to the realization that I didn't enjoy the field and was not looking forward to my career. Fortunately, I had a couple of professors who liked me and recognized my hard work ethic. Using their own contacts, they helped me to get a job in computer software development for a major defense contractor. My new career choice is much better suited to my personality and interests. Best of all, my employer is paying for me to continue my education in the computer field."

Ray
Software Developer

"I had been at home for years. I'd always followed my husband's career and needed to be available to entertain important business guests, organize my husband's travels, and research the never-ending array of new hometowns. Eventually, I decided I needed a career of my own. I was terrified and felt low on self-confidence and experience. With the help of a career counselor, I developed a wonderful functional résumé that stressed my organizational and hospitality skills as well as my experience with international guests. I now work for a major hotel as an events planner and have really utilized my life's experience and skills."

Sylvie
Events Planner

"I'd always worked summer jobs at our local beach. When I was in high school, a seasonal position at the ice cream stand or hotel front desk seemed convenient, if not especially educational. During rainy days I really minded the slow times and hated waiting around for a customer to come in. Something interesting happened, though.

Since I often worked alone in the evenings, the patrol officers on beat would often check in on me to make sure everything was okay. Anxious for conversation, I began to pass the time by asking them about their day and the job. Soon, I have a new group of friends and some real insights into the daily duties of a police officer. I decided to use that summer income to get a degree in criminal justice. Now I'm the one checking in on the summer help."

Michelle
Police Officer

"My little girl was born prematurely, necessitating a long stay in the hospital. I spent hours rocking her in the hospital nursery in the evenings. I came to know the nurses on the floor. I listened to them talk with each other, I watched what duties they had on their shifts, and asked them a lot of questions. After my daughter was well, we occasionally returned to the hospital for a visit. The nurses on duty encouraged me to investigate careers in nursing. When my child started preschool, I took a position as a nurse's aid. I learned of scholarships available to those planning to enter a career in nursing. Today, I proudly wear the title of registered nurse after my name."

Tracy
Registered Nurse

"I took a work-study job with the buildings and grounds department at the college I attended. I loved the work because I got a chance to solve all sorts of maintenance problems for every department at the school. The CAD department needed a lot of help planning and installing some new cabinetry in their new office space, and I came to know everyone there really well. I got my degree in architectural design and my first job as CAD manager for the campus."

Chris
Architect

"I was working as a nurse for a pediatrician. One day another nurse came into the office and asked the pediatrician I worked for to precept, or mentor, her through her nurse practitioner program. The doctor replied, 'If I were going to precept ANYONE, it would be Marilyn.' I looked up in disbelief. I had never considered going on for an advanced degree, and had no idea that my employer would be so supportive. I seized the opportunity, took him up on his offer, and am now very satisfied with my job as a nurse practitioner."

Marilyn
Nurse Practitioner

EXERCISE EXERCISE

1. Having read through these success stories, what themes emerge? What can you learn from the experiences of these individuals?

2. Think of your own friends and family. How did they get their jobs?

3. Write down the names of at least three people you know who hold jobs that you think are interesting.

1. _____

2. _____

3. _____

4. Within the next few days, contact those people and ask them how they obtained their jobs. What can you learn from the experiences of these individuals?

Advice from Those Who've Made It

Many of the people we spoke to in writing *The Ultimate Job Hunter's Guidebook* were willing to share advice about job hunting and career success. Here, briefly, are some of the thoughts that emerged most frequently:

1. To succeed, choose a career you love.

2. Keep your eyes open for any and every opportunity. Then go for it!

3. Make your own breaks.

4. Learn something from every task and every job. It all comes in handy someday in some way you can't foresee at the time.

5. Nobody is indispensable, especially you.

6. Learn from all the people you meet. Everyone has some special quality, skill, or talent.

7. Every problem is an opportunity in disguise.

8. Don't sweat the small stuff, and remember, most stuff is small.

9. Seek out challenges. Your greatest personal satisfaction will come from difficult achievements.

10. Take setbacks in stride. Learn from your failures.

11. Don't make the same mistake twice.

12. Cultivate your talents. Work on improving your deficiencies.

13. Persistence will get you almost anything eventually.

14. Try to make the right decisions in life. Rectify wrong decisions as hastily as possible.

15. Don't get caught up in the day-to-day stresses. Focus on the positive aspects of the big picture.

16. Work toward long-term goals, but enjoy life today.

17. Become the most positive and enthusiastic person you know.

18. Be decisive, even if it means you'll sometimes by wrong.

19. Commit yourself to becoming a lifelong learner.

20. Character counts.

21. Be a nice person.

As you embark on your career, you'll be creating your own "success stories" and developing your own ideas about how to advance in the work place. Write to us about your experiences. We'd love to hear about them and possibly even include them in the next edition of *The Ultimate Job Hunter's Guidebook*. Be sure to include your name, address, and phone number so we can contact you.

Send submissions to:

Houghton Mifflin Company, College Business Division
222 Berkeley Street
Boston, MA 02116

or to our e-mail address:

college_bus@hmco.com.

INDEX

Abbreviations, 28, 116
Abstract skills, 32
Acceptance letters, 180–182
Achievement profile keys,
  140–141
Action verbs, 27, 30–31
Action without Borders, 81
Activities, 26
Addenda, to résumés, 53
AltaVista, 90, 93
America Online, 89
Anxiety, 134–135
Assertiveness, 63
Assets, 10–11
Attire. *See* Personal grooming

Beethoven, Ludwig von, 219
Behavioral interviews, 123
Better Business Bureau, 68
Biographies, 53
Blind ads, 63–64
Board interviews, 123–124
Body, in cover letters, 96
Body language, 142–143
The Book for the States, 73
Bureau of Labor Statistics, 200
Business cards, job-search, 53
Business etiquette, 126–127

Capitalization, 25
Career America Connection, 79
Career coaches, 20
Career counselors, 20, 173–174
Career Counselors Consortium,
  20
Career Development Services
  (Rochester, N.Y.), 20
Career discussion groups,
  on-line, 90
Career Experience, 20
Career goals, 16–18
Career tests, 20

Career trends, 200–202
CareerPath.com, 91–92
Chambers of commerce, 68–69
Chronological résumés
  examples of, 35–40
  explanation of, 33
  gaps in job history in, 52
  revision of, 47
Churchill, Winston, 219
Classified ads
  letters in response to, 101,
    107, 108
  miscellaneous sources of,
    64–65
  placed by employment
    agencies, 64
  for positions wanted, 59
  responses to, 63, 65
  types of, 63–64
Closing, in cover letters, 96
College placement offices, 163
Communication
  body language as, 142–143
  with managers, 190
  on-the-job, 188
Community colleges, 202, 203
Competitors, 68
Compressed work weeks, 195
Computer software, 54
Computer use, 78, 206. *See also*
  Internet
Concrete skills, 32
Contractors, 162
Corporate culture, 185, 190
Cousy, Bob, 219
Cover letters. *See also* Letters
  alternative strategies for,
    100–101
  elements of, 96
  function of, 4–5
  importance of, 96
  sample, 101–108

scannable, 54–56, 98
  tips for writing, 97–100
  types of, 101
Coworker relationships, 190–192

Databases, 54, 56, 64
Deductive order, 100
Deja News, 90
Department of Commerce, 79
Dinner interviews, 124
Directed interviews, 124
Disney, Walt, 219
Display ads, 63
Distributors, 68
Drug tests, 154

E-mail, 59, 92
Edison, Thomas, 219
Education
  for federal jobs, 77
  importance of continuing,
    206, 208
  need for further, 85–86, 193
  opportunities to further,
    193–194
  on résumés, 26
  two-year degrees and, 202,
    203
Einstein, Albert, 219
Employer Profiles, 90
Employers. *See* Potential
  employers
Employment agencies
  classified ads placed by, 64
  fee payments to, 59, 64
  interviews at, 161
  for temporary positions,
    160–161
  use of, 59
Employment tests
  drug tests as, 154
  physical, 157

Employment tests (*con't*)
  psychological tests as, 155–157
  skills tests as, 154–155
  types of, 5
Entrepreneurship. *See*
  Self-employment
Entry-level jobs, 162–163
Etiquette
  business, 126–127
  telephone, 129, 188
Ex-employees, 69
Excite, 89, 93
Executive search firms, 60

Faxes, 59
Federal jobs
  overview of, 77
  reasons to consider, 77
  sources for locating, 77–79
  types of, 77
Financial data, 68
Five O'Clock Club, 20
Flextime, 195
Freelance work, 162
Functional résumés
  examples of, 41–43
  explanation of, 33–34
  gaps in job history in, 52
  revision of, 48

Galaxy, 93
Gender, pay gap and, 80
Grooming. *See* Personal
  grooming
Group interviews, 124
Growth firms, 59

Hoover's Online, 90
HotBot, 93

I, in résumés, 27
Illegal questions, 138
Inductive order, 100
Informational interviews
  function of, 124
  generating job leads by, 59
  guidelines for, 70
  sample questions for, 71
  thank-you letters following,
    70, 72

Infoseek, 93
Interests
  identifying your, 137–138
  on résumés, 26
Internet
  access to, 89
  benefits of job hunting using,
    88–89
  career discussion groups on,
    90
  career guidance sites on, 92
  electronic bulletin boards on,
    91
  entrepreneurial sites on, 83
  explanation of, 88
  finding internships on, 163
  guidelines for using, 92–94
  job hunting and career sites
    on, 92, 94
  job listings on, 60, 79, 90
  on-line newspaper classified
    sections on, 91–92
  posting personal web page
    on, 92
  posting résumés, 54, 57, 90
  researching companies using,
    67–68, 90
  researching nonprofit
    organizations using, 80, 81
  salary information on,
    178–179
  search engines and, 89, 90, 93
Internships, 163–164
Interviewers
  potential questions asked by,
    135–137
  questions to ask, 138–139
  types of, 122
Interviews
  body language during,
    142–143
  business etiquette for, 126–127
  creating good first impression
    on, 125
  at employment agencies, 161
  handling rejection following,
    150–151
  handling stress during,
    132–135
  illegal questions during, 138

informational, 59, 70–72
  nontraditional ways to
    obtain, 147
  overview of, 5
  personal grooming for,
    127–128
  potential questions you
    might be asked during,
    135–138
  preparation for, 122–123
  profile keys during, 139–142
  questions to ask interviewer
    during, 138–139
  reasons for unsuccessful,
    148–150
  self-evaluation following,
    143–144
  telephone, 130–131
  telephone presentation to
    obtain, 128–130
  thank-you letters following,
    70, 72, 145
  types of, 123–124
Introductory paragraphs, 96
Inverted pyramid style, 100
Italics, on résumés, 25

Job applications
  guidelines for filling out,
    116–117
  information for, 5
  sample, 119–120
  typical questions on, 117–118
Job fairs, 65–67
Job history, 52–53
Job leads, 59–60
Job offers
  acceptance letter following,
    180–182
  evaluating, 6, 176–178
  negotiating salary following,
    178–180
  rejection letter following, 182,
    183
Job satisfaction, 199
Job search
  advice for, 222–223
  keeping goals in mind
    during, 151–152, 168–169
  long-distance, 74–75

organization chart for, 146
organizing and surviving, 6,
 167–174
relocating for purpose of,
 73–74
steps in, 2–6
success stories in, 211–221
troubleshooting during,
 172–173
Job-search business cards, 53
Job security, 203–204
Job-shadowing, 18
Job sharing, 195
Jobs
 changing direction in, 84–85
 entry-level, 162–163
 in federal government, 77–79
 first weeks on, 185
 first year on, 185–189
 freelance, 162
 future outlook for, 6
 holding multiple, 159–160
 internship, 163–164
 in local government, 79
 in nonprofit organizations,
  79–81
 overseas, 74–75
 part-time, 198
 in small companies, 81
 temporary, 160–162, 198
 trends in, 200–202
 volunteer, 164–165
 when to move on from,
  195–196
Jordan, Michael, 219

Keywords, 56–57

Labor force trends, 198–199,
 205, 207
Language. *See also*
 Communication
 on-the-job, 188
 on résumés, 27–28
Lead-generating letters, 101,
 103, 104
Letters. *See also* Cover letters
 to accept positions, 180–182
 following interviews, 70, 72,
  145

formats for, 97
lead-generating, 101, 103, 104
of recommendation, 5,
 110–114
to reject positions, 181, 183
in response to classified ads,
 101, 107, 108
sample, 101–108
styles for, 100–101
types of, 101
Libraries, 69
Lincoln, Abraham, 214
List style, 100–101
Liszt Select, 89, 90
Local government jobs, 79
Long-distance job hunting,
 74–75
Longenecker, C. W., 218
Lunch interviews, 124
Lycos, 93

Managers, 189–190
Medical examinations, 157
Mentors, 192
Municipal Yearbook, 73
Myer-Briggs, 20

Narrative résumés, 53
Networking
 approaches to, 69
 to find internships, 163–164
 generating job leads by, 59
 importance of, 208
 making charts to keep track
  of, 60–62
 in professional organizations,
  60, 193–194
 at seminars or conferences,
  193–194
 in volunteer positions, 19
Networking groups, 194
Newsletter editors, 59
Newspapers
 on-line classified sections of,
  91–92
 researching potential
  employers using, 68
Newton, Sir Isaac, 219
Nondirected interviews, 124
Nonprofit Career Network, 81

Nonprofit organizations
 locating information about, 80
 locating jobs in, 81
 overview of, 79–80
 pay gap between men and
  women in, 80
 volunteer positions in, 164
Nouns, 56
Numbers, in résumés, 28

*The Occupational Outlook
 Handbook,* 200
Occupations
 changing direction in, 84–85
 fastest growing, 201, 202
 trends in, 200–202
Office of Personnel
 Management, 77, 79
On-line résumés, 54–57
Opportunity NOCs, 81
Organization chart, 146
Overseas jobs, 74–75

Paper, for résumés, 24–25
Part-time employment, 198
Performance reviews, 192–193
Personal grooming
 for filling out job applications
  on-site, 116–117
 for interviews, 127–128
 for job fairs, 66
 on-the-job, 187
Personal profile keys, 139–140
Personal web pages, 92
Personality traits, 139–141
Philanthropy Journal Online, 81
Physical agility tests, 157
*The Plum Book (United States
 Government Policy and
 Supporting Positions),* 79
Polygraph tests, 156
Potential employers
 assertiveness in dealing with,
  63
 classified ads placed by, 63–65
 conducting research on,
  67–69, 90
 guidelines for generating
  leads to, 59–60
 importance of targeting, 4

Potential employers (*con't*)
  informational interviews to
    identify, 70–72
  job fairs as source of, 65–67
  long-distance hunting to
    identify, 74–75
  miscellaneous job listings by,
    64–65
  networking to find, 60–62, 69
  relocation to find, 73–74
  telephone calls to, 59, 128–129
Probation period, 157
Problem/solution style, 100
Products, 68
Profanity, 188
Professional organizations, 60,
    193–194. *See also* Nonprofit
    organizations; Trade
    organizations
Professional profile keys, 140
Profile keys, 139–141
Promotions, 59
Psychological tests, 155–157
Punctuation, 25

Recommendation letters
  content of, 111
  example of, 114
  function of, 5
  number of, 111
  process of obtaining, 110–111
  sample letter to request, 113
  sources for, 110
  when to submit, 111–112
References
  for job application, 116
  requests for, 110–111
  résumés and availability of,
    26, 112
  who to list as, 110
Referral letters, 101, 105, 106
Rejection, 150–151
Rejection letters, 181, 183
Relaxation techniques, 133
Relocation
  for potential jobs, 73–74
  salary information and, 178
Research, on potential
    employers, 67–69, 90
Résumé scanning software, 54

Résumés
  alternatives to, 53–54
  basic elements of, 25–26
  chronological, 33, 35–40, 47,
    52
  computer-friendly, 54–57
  on databases, 54, 56, 65
  dos and don'ts for, 28–30
  facts about, 22–24
  format for, 25
  functional, 33–34, 41–43, 48,
    52
  job history gaps in, 52–53
  language used for, 27–28
  listing skills on, 32
  narrative, 53
  paper used for, 24–25
  preparation of, 3
  revision of, 44–48
  software for, 54
  verb use in, 27, 30–31, 56
  what not to write in, 27
  worksheet for, 49–52
Ruth, Babe, 219

Salary
  in fast-growing occupations,
    202
  guidelines for negotiating,
    178–180
  Internet sites to research,
    178–179
  job applications and, 116
  performance review and,
    193
  research on, 92
  for temporary positions, 161
Search engines, 89, 90, 93
Search.com, 93
Self-assessment
  to aid in choosing right job,
    14–16
  evaluating priorities as
    element of, 13–14
  function of, 3
  gaining knowledge for, 8–11
  setting career goals following,
    16–18
  taking positive moves
    following, 12–13

Self-employment
  exploring possibilities of,
    83–84
  positive and negative aspects
    of, 82–83
Self-evaluation, 143–144
Seminars, 193
The Service Corps of Retired
    Executives, 83
Sexual harassment, 188
Situational interviews, 123
Skills, 32
Skills tests, 154–155
Slang, 188
Small Business Administration,
    83
Small companies, 81
Smart Business Supersite, 83
Specific skills, 32
State employment offices, 60
Straight classified ads, 63
Stress
  finding outlets for, 169
  during interviews, 132–135
  management of, 133
Stress interviews, 124
Strong Interest Inventory, 20
Suppliers, 68
Svoboda's Home & Small
    Business Interactive, 83

Teams, 208–209
Telecommuting, 195
Telegraphic phrases, 27
Telephone calls
  etiquette for, 129, 188
  to potential employers, 59,
    128–129
Telephone interviews, 124,
    130–131
Temporary agencies, 160
Temporary employment,
    160–162, 198
Tests. *See also* Employment
    tests
  career, 20
  drug, 154
  physical, 157
  psychological, 155–157
  skills, 154–155

Thank-you letters
  following interviews, 70, 72, 145
  following job search, 185
Time management
  do lists for, 168, 170
  during job search, 167–168
  time planning lists for, 171
Trade organizations
  networking in, 60
  researching potential employers at meetings of, 68
  seminars and conferences sponsored by, 193–194
Trade publications
  checking web sites of, 89
  locating information on nonprofit organizations using, 80
  researching potential employers using, 68

salary information published in, 178
Trade shows, 68
Trends
  career success tips based on, 206, 208–209
  in growth occupations, 200–202
  in job openings, 200, 204–205
  in job security, 203–204
  in labor force, 198–199, 205, 207
  in two-year degrees, 202–203
  in work arrangements, 194–195
Troubleshooting, 172–173

Underlining, 25
United States Government Policy and Supporting Positions (The Plum Book), 79

United Way, 80
U.S. Census Data, 73

Venture capital companies, 59
Verbs, 27, 30–31, 56
Voice stress analysis, 156
Volunteer Center Directory, 165
Volunteer work, 19, 164–165

Wages. *See* Salary
Wall Street Journal, 20
Woolworth, F. W., 219
Work arrangements, 194–195
Work samples, 53–54
Work schedules, 195
World Wide Web. *See* Internet

Yahoo!, 89, 93
Yellow Pages, 60, 160